Aladdin and his Wonderful Lamp

A Victorian Pantomime

Alan Brown

A Samuel French Acting Edition

SAMUELFRENCH-LONDON.CO.UK
SAMUELFRENCH.COM

Copyright © 1991 by Alan Brown
All Rights Reserved

ALADDIN AND HIS WONDERFUL LAMP is fully protected under the copyright laws of the British Commonwealth, including Canada, the United States of America, and all other countries of the Copyright Union. All rights, including professional and amateur stage productions, recitation, lecturing, public reading, motion picture, radio broadcasting, television and the rights of translation into foreign languages are strictly reserved.

ISBN 978-0-573-06486-9

www.samuelfrench-london.co.uk

www.samuelfrench.com

For Amateur Production Enquiries

United Kingdom and World
excluding north america

plays@SamuelFrench-London.co.uk

020 7255 4302/01

Each title is subject to availability from Samuel French,
depending upon country of performance.

CAUTION: Professional and amateur producers are hereby warned that ALADDIN AND HIS WONDERFUL LAMP is subject to a licensing fee. Publication of this play does not imply availability for performance. Both amateurs and professionals considering a production are strongly advised to apply to the appropriate agent before starting rehearsals, advertising, or booking a theatre. A licensing fee must be paid whether the title is presented for charity or gain and whether or not admission is charged.

The professional rights in this play are controlled by Samuel French Ltd, 52 Fitzroy Street, London, W1T 5JR.

No one shall make any changes in this title for the purpose of production. No part of this book may be reproduced, stored in a retrieval system, or transmitted in any form, by any means, now known or yet to be invented, including mechanical, electronic, photocopying, recording, videotaping, or otherwise, without the prior written permission of the publisher. No one shall upload this title, or part of this title, to any social media websites.

The right of Alan Brown to be identified as author of this work has been asserted by him in accordance with Section 77 of the Copyright, Designs and Patents Act 1988

CHARACTERS

Aladdin, a scamp with a lamp
Widow Twanky, his mother, a Chinese laundry-woman
Wishee-Washee, his step-brother, a laundry-boy
Abanazar, an Arabian magician
The Emperor of China, the biggest pot in the Land of Tea
Princess Badroulbadour, his daughter, the dear object of Aladdin's affections
Swee-Tee ⎫
Ainchee-Nice ⎭ her "maids in waiting"
Vizier, another top pot in China

Ping ⎫
Pong ⎭ the Peking constabulary
*Ermintrude, a talented camel
Citizens of Peking

Immortals

Slave of The Ring ⎫ Genii
Slave of the Lamp ⎭
**The Dragon, a magic oracle
Fiery Spirits and Goblins

The Harlequinade:

Harlequin (Slave of the Lamp)
Columbine (Slave of the Ring)
Pantaloon (Ping)
Clown (Pong)
Butcher (Citizen)
"Blossom" (Ermintrude)

*Can be doubled with other characters.
**Voice only, could be doubled with Emperor.

SYNOPSIS OF SCENES

PART I
SCENE 1   The magic cave of the Dragon Oracle
SCENE 2   A street in old Peking
SCENE 3   Outside the magic cave
SCENE 4   Inside the magic cave

PART II
SCENE 5   Widow Twanky's laundry
SCENE 6   The Emperor's palace
SCENE 7   In front of Aladdin's palace
SCENE 8   Pursuit of the flying palace through the air
SCENE 9   Inside Aladdin's palace in Africa
SCENE 10 Outside the palace

PRODUCTION NOTE

To set the period it is suggested that during the arrival of the audience an advertisement cloth is displayed bearing 1890's period advertisements by local shops and firms still in existence today. Immediately prior to the rise of the Curtain the advertisement cloth is raised, and a Victorian stage manager comes from behind the Curtain with a lighted taper and ignites the (imitation) footlights.

MUSICAL NUMBERS

The lyrics to songs printed in the text are from non-copyright works (although in two instances the music was copyright at the time of printing). Titles of other, copyright, works to be used are included in the full list, printed below. Please remember, however, that a licence issued by Samuel French Ltd to perform this pantomime does NOT include permission to use copyright songs and music. Please read the notice supplied by the Performing Right Society on page ix.

PART I

Overture		
Song 1	*Chin Chin Chinaman* by Sidney Jones from *The Geisha**	Chorus
Song 2	*Two Lovely Black Eyes* by Coborn and Forman	Wishee-Washee
Song 3	*Entrance of the Emperor* by Sidney Jones from *San Toy*	Chorus
Song 4	*I Mean To Introduce It Into China!* by Sidney Jones*	Emperor and Chorus
Song 5	*Waiting At The Church* by F. W. Leigh and H. E. Penther	Widow Twanky
Song 6	*Hold Your Hand Out, You Naughty Boy!* by Murphy and David	Aladdin and Company
Song 7	*Ask A P'liceman* by Rogers and Durandeau†	Ping and Pong
Song 8	*Boiled Beef and Carrots* by Collins and Murray	Aladdin, Wishee-Washee and Widow Twanky
Song 9	*None Shall Peep!* after "Nessum Dorma" from *Turandot* by Puccini	Ping (or Pong) and Company
Song 10	*Let Me Call You Sweetheart* by Whitsun and Friedman	Aladdin and Princess
Song 11	*Ask a P'liceman* (reprise)	Princess, Ping, Pong, Swee-Tee, Ainchee
Music 11a	Dance: to the music of *The Carnival of the Animals* by Saint Saens	
Song 12	*Down With You Quickly!* to the air of *Down Went McGinty* by J. Flynn	Abanazar and Aladdin
Music 12a	Dance: to *Le Rouet d'Omphale* by Saint Saens	

Song 13	Dance of the Fiery Spirits to the theme of *Danse Macabre* by Saint Saens	

PART II

Song 14	*The Chinese Laundrymen* by C. G. Cotes and Benet Scott	Chorus
Song 15	*Who Threw the Overalls in Widow Twanky's Chowder?* by G. L. Geifer	Wishee-Washee and Company
Song 16	*Where Is My Wandering Boy Tonight?* by Rev. R. Lowry[†]	Widow Twanky and Company
Song 17	*Like the Big Pots Do!* by J. P. Long	Widow Twanky, Wishee-Washee and Aladdin
Song 18	*The Man Who Broke the Bank at Monte Carlo* by Fred Gilbert	Emperor and Company
Music 18a	Music: *Beautiful Galathea*	
Song 19	*Let Me Call You Sweetheart* (reprise)	Princess, Aladdin, Company and Chorus
Song 20	*Why Am I Always the Bridesmaid?*	Swee-Tee and Ainchee-Nice
Song 21	*For Old Things I'm Now Exchanging* to the air of "Serenade" from *Faust* (Gounod)	Abanazar
Music 21a	Music: *Ride of the Valkyries*	
Song 22	*A Bird In A Gilded Cage*	Princess and Goblins
Song 23	*Oh, Abanazar* to the melody of "Oh, Mr Porter" by T. & G. Brunn	Widow Twanky, Wishee, Vizier, Emperor, Aladdin, Swee-Tee, Ainchee-Nice
Song 24	*Let Me Call You Sweetheart* (reprise)	Company

*The music is copyright for this song.
[†]No information available from PRS regarding copyright position.

The following statement concerning the use of music is printed here on behalf of the Performing Right Society Ltd, by whom it was supplied

The permission of the owner of the performing right in copyright music must be obtained before any public performance may be given, whether in conjunction with a play or sketch or otherwise, and this permission is just as necessary for amateur performances as for professional. The majority of copyright musical works (other than oratorios, musical plays and similar dramatico-musical works) are controlled in the British Commonwealth by the PERFORMING RIGHT SOCIETY LTD, 29–33 BERNERS STREET, LONDON W1P 4AA.

The society's practice is to issue licences authorizing the use of its repertoire to the proprietors of premises at which music is publicly performed, or, alternatively, to the organizers of musical entertainments, but the Society does not require payment of fees by performers as such. Producers or promoters of plays, sketches, etc., at which music is to be performed, during or after the play or sketch, should ascertain whether the premises at which their performances are to be given are covered by a licence issued by the Society, and if they are not, should make application to the Society for particulars as to the fee payable.

To
Ron Baskerville
and
Barry Jarvis
—for the "annual miracle"

PART I

Scene I

The magic cave of the dragon oracle

There is a bright green flash with smoke. Abanazar appears. He wears an elaborate turban and is dressed in Arabic fashion

Abanazar Soho, my friends! Don't leave your seats!
There's no cause for alarm.
Though I've arrived from warmer spheres
I mean you all no harm.
I am a fraud, fearful fraud!
As bad as I can be,
In fact, I'm up to ev'ry dodge,
You must have heard of me.
I am Abanazar,—hear the children cry!
They run away like frightened sheep
When I come creeping by.
See them shake and tremble!
Where'er this wizard roams,
And people shout "It's him! Look out!"
And run back in their homes!

A gigantic red Chinese dragon's head, with large glowing eyes, and smoke belching from its angry mouth, appears

Dragon Who dares disturb the spirits of my cave,
The guardians of the Flame, and faithful slaves
Of our great conflagration? Would you spy
Upon our fiery secrets? You shall die!

Smoke billows from the Dragon's mouth

Abanazar Not so! Let me explain my true position.
I am one Abanazar, a magician——
By the Gods condemnéd with a curse
One thousand years to roam the universe.
On Queen Victoria's reign I've now descended——
Dragon And how are things on Earth?
Abanazar   Oh, splendid! splendid!
Strikes, pollution, poverty and crime,
Rogues growing rich, while honest men "do time".
Back to the wall the strong ones thrust the weak,
And nothing scores save impudence and cheek.

Since greed is then the fashion I would be
Ruler of this world!
Dragon   What do you wish of me?
Abanazar I seek throughout the earth a lamp, long hidden,
To find it I by avarice am driven.
Who holds that priceless treasure in his hand
Illimitable power may command.
Help me to find the magic lamp that's lost,
I would possess its power at any cost.
My wealth's colossal, any price I'll pay
To gain the lamp. Speak! It is far away?
Dragon Far, far away, within a magic cave,
Protected by guardian sprite and slave.
Abanazar But whereabouts?
Dragon   The magic lamp you're seeking
Lies in a cave in China,—outside Peking.
To gain an entrance to that cavern drear
Repeat the magic words which now you hear.
Voices of the Spirits Abracadabra, Abracadee,
Magical Cavern open to me——
Open, oh open, great Sesame!
Abanazar "Open Sesame!"

Thunder

Dragon But you shall waste your time and trouble too.
No evil soul can enter there like you,
For he who enters there must be a youth
Whose lips ne'er uttered aught but words of truth.
Abanazar That quaint description I don't answer to,
Nor can I think *who* it exactly fits! Can you?
Speak! Oracle of Fire! To me reveal
Whose hand may reach the treasure I would steal?
Dragon Aladdin is the boy that Fates shall give
That power.
Abanazar   *Aladdin*? Where does this brat live?
Dragon He dwells in Peking, and it is decreed
By him alone the lamp's charms shall be freed.
Voices of the Spirits Aladdin! Aladdin!
Aladdin the bold,
Treasure awaits him
In silver and gold.

The Dragon's head disappears

Abanazar (*speaking through the chorus, aside*)
Aladdin! I shall not forget his name!
They say he's but a boy,—that suits my game!
I'll find Aladdin,—get the lamp from *him*,
He'll find his chances of reward are slim,

Part I, Scene 2

But how? We'll have to summon, I'm afraid,
The Demon County Council to our aid.
Spite! Envy! Hatred! Malice! Aid my plan.
Come with me, all ye vices, to a man!
Before the day has sped another hour
That frisky youngster shall be in my power,
The lamp be mine, its magic powers unfurl'd,
And I alone the Ruler of the World!

Abanazar exits

Thunder. Lightning

Black-out

Frontcloth removed to reveal ...

SCENE 2

A street in Old Peking

Dominant is "Widow Twanky's laundry", on the front of which is a door marked "In", the end of a laundry chute coming through the wall marked "Out", and a door marked "Exit". Beneath the name of the laundry is a notice reading: "Articles washed, steamed, and pressed". Outside the "in" door is a notice: "Leave your shoes here". There is also a small practical window

Other shop signs in the street include "Shod-Hi" Clothing Mart, "Chow-Chow" Dining Rooms, "Oh-Mi" Curiosities, "Dress-Sing" Milliner, "Chin-Chin" Barbers, "Ketchi-Ketchi" Fishmonger. To one side is a Victorian pillar box

In front of the laundry pickets are walking in a circle, three of them are holding placards which read: "Laundlee no Pay Ploper Wagee!", "While Strikee-Strikee——", and, "Iron Not Hottee!"

Song 1: Chin Chin Chinaman

Pickets   Chinaman no money makee
                 Allo Lifee Long!
                 Washee-washee if we takee
                 Oh, by Goshee, wrong!
                 When we thinkee stealee collars
                 P'licee-manee come;
                 We get finee fivee dollars,
                 Plenty muchee sum!
                 Chin Chin Chinaman
                 Muchee muchee sad,

| | We aflaid allo trade
Wellee wellee bad.
No-ee joke,
Brokee-broke,
Makee shuttee shop!
Chin Chin Chinaman
Chop! chop! chop! |
| -------------- | --- |
| Everyone | Chin Chin Chinaman
Muchee muchee sad!
Etc., etc. |
| 1st Picket | When we gettee catchee cheatee
Playing piecee card,
P'licee-men they also beatee,
Kickee wellee hard!
When we takee nicee placee
Makee plenty tea,
Gettee we in more disglacee,
Up they sellee we! |
| Everyone | Chin chin Chinaman
Muchee muchee sad,
We aflaid allo trade
Wellee wellee bad.
No-ee joke,
Brokee-broke,
Makee shuttee shop!
Chin chin Chinaman
Chop! chop! chop! |
| Everyone | Chin chin Chinaman
Muchee muchee sad,
Etc., etc. |

At the end of the number they open the laundry basket to reveal Wishee. He has two large "black" eyes

Everyone (*stamping their feet in unison*)
   Oh, Wishee-Washee! Wakey! Wakey! Wishee-Washee!
1st Picket When missie come, she settle all your hashee!
2nd Picket No rice and choppee-sticks for you today!
3rd Picket When you no workee you will get no pay!
Wishee Me strikee strikee. Want more pay for washee!
   Because old missie, she keep all my cashee!
4th Picket Upon your lazy backee precious quickee
   You'll get a taste of missie bamboo stickee!
1st Picket If you go strikee and no workee you
   Will quickly feel old missie can strike too!
2nd Picket What happened to both eyeball, Wishee-Washee?
Wishee Wishee crossee picket line, by goshee!
   Home Rule for China cannot be denied!
3rd Picket Then Chamberlain commit chop-sueyside!

Part I, Scene 2

All groan

Song 2: Two Lovely Black Eyes

Wishee	Strolling this morning in old Peking Young Wishee-Washee you might have seen, Joey and I with old Bill between——
All	Oh, what a surprise!
Wishee	I plaised the Conserlative flank and flee Old Joey got angly so speed-i-lee, All in a moment he handed to me Two lovely black eyes!
Wishee	Two lovely black eyes, Oh! What a surplise! Only for telling a man he was wrong! Two lovely black eyes!
	Next time I argued I thought it best To give the "Conserlative" side a lest, The melits of Gladstone I fleely pless'd, When, oh! what a surplise! The chap I had met was a Torly tlue, Nothing the Libelals light could do, This was my share of that argument too, Two lovely black eyes!

A Victorian Stage Manager enters with the words of the chorus on an easel

Wishee and the Chorus invite the audience to join in

Everyone	Two lovely black eyes, Oh! What a surplise! Only for telling a man he was wrong! Two lovely black eyes!
Wishee	The molal you've caught I can hardly doubt, Never in politics lave and shout, Leave it to others to fight it out, If you would be wise. Better, far better, it is to let Lib'lals and Torlies alone, you bet, Unless you're willing and anxious to get Two lovely black eyes!
Everyone	Two lovely black eyes, Etc., etc.

Repeat the Chorus

  At the end of the chorus Wishee-Washee exits

Trumpets sound a fanfare. Gong!

Citizen The Emperor!
All The Emperor!!

Song 3

The Emperor and Vizier enter

Emperor Dear people. "How dee do?"
Citizens How dee do!
Emperor Welcome to this meeting
  Whilst on my tour I have picked up this English way of greeting
  I had a splendid trip, just as I always do,
  I went to Richmond, Hampton Court, to Hampstead and to Kew.
Vizier (*sadly*) Also to Kempton Park!
Emperor You're right, and hence the topper!
  I learnt in England to behave in ways extremely proper!

Song 4: I Mean To Introduce It Into China

(*Singing*)   I used to think a Chinaman
    Was twenty times as fine a man
    As any born of European nations.
    Our manners were superior
    To anything exterior,
    And had been so for many generations.
    But now there's not a doubt of it
    That China will be out of it
    Unless we can effect a vast improvement.
    We'll copy the variety
    Of English high society,
    And I will be the leader of the movement.
    So we'll emulate the styles
    Of the blessed British Isles,
    Though the reason isn't easy to define—Ah!
    But they do it in the West,
    So of course it must be best,
    And I mean to introduce it into China.
Everyone   So we'll emulate the styles
    Of the blessed British Isles
    Etc., etc.
    (And *he* means to introduce it into China.)
Vizier How did you like Brighton, your Majesty?
Emperor Frightfully expensive! I made a sandcastle on the beach, and ten minutes later a fellow from the Council came up and wanted to charge me poll tax! We stayed at a little boarding house only a stone's throw from the beach. It was easy to find—all the windows were broken! (*He claps his hands*)

Part I, Scene 2

A girl dressed in a saucy can-can costume comes forward

(*Singing*) In 'Gay Paree' ... (I fancy so) I saw a girl who dances so
That foreign devils think her most diverting!

The girl dances. Other girls gather round her and gradually emulate her steps until they too are dancing in unison with her

                    She pirouetted gracefully,
With skirts expanding lacefully,
At first I found it highly disconcerting!
But soon I grew so used to her,
That I was introduced to her,
And asked her to assist our reformation.
She'll teach our pit and gallery,
At quite a princely salary,
The proper course of female education!
Though the dances you will see
May be thought a trifle free
Yet she knows exactly where to draw the line—Ah!
And she's reckoned quite the best
In the Empire of the West,
So I mean to introduce her into China!

Everyone Though the dances you will see
May be thought a trifle free
Etc., etc.

They begin to exit

So we'll emulate the styles
Of the blessed British Isles
Though the reasons isn't easy to divine,—Ah!
But they do it in the West,
So of course it must be best,
And he means to intro-duce it into China!

They exit

Steam and pandemonium inside the laundry, followed by an explosion. Widow Twanky comes flying down the laundry chute amidst a pile of laundry

Widow Twanky Great Crispy Noodles! My nerves are quite upset!
And so was I! I don't feel steady yet!

She staggers to her feet

That wretched chute—to pitch me in the gutter!
Where's me drop of mother's ruin?
            Ah! Underneath me shutter!

She raises her apron, and takes out a bottle of gin

A little lotion to allay the pain!

She drinks, puts some on her fingers which she applies behind her ears, shakes some under her armpits, pours some into one ear and blows it out through her lips

Ah! That's better! Twanky is herself again! ... Oh, by the way, that's me name. Do forgive me, I haven't introduced myself. Twanky! Widow Twanky! I expect you know who you are! No, please don't get up. ... 'Evening squire! ... Ah, the men! God bless 'em! What would we do without them, eh Ladies? Oh yes, and I've had me moments too, you know. As a matter of fact I've buried two husbands. I have! I've buried two husbands! Well I had to, see love,—they died! So!—who have we got in tonight? (*She peers into the auditorium and finds a child*) Hello, there's a pretty little girl down there. What's your name, love? ... That's a lovely name! Where do you come from? ... Oh yes! That'll be a nice place when it's finished! How old are you? ... And are you married yet? ... No? You don't want to be left on the shelf, you know. Have you started your bottom drawer yet? No?! Here, we'll need to get you gingered up. Now let's see. Who have we got over here? (*She peers into the auditorium on the other side of the house*) I say! Here's a handsome young man down here. (*To a little boy*) What's your name, love? ... Where do you come from? ... (*Local gag, in period*) ... And how old are you? ... !! (*To a little girl*) I've got just the man for you, duck! Catch 'em when they're young. And he must have a bob or two sitting in the posh seats up the front here. (*To boy*) Now here's what you do young "———" (*Boy's Name*) During the interval, you go and meet young "———" (*Girl's Name*) and then you can buy her a great big ice-cream. Will you? Will you do that? ... No?! What do you mean "No!"? Isn't that a typical man? Oh, never mind, perhaps he's poor. Are you poor, love? I know what it's like to be poor. You know, when we were kids we were so poor my Mummy couldn't afford to buy me shoes. Do you know what she used to do? She used to paint me feet black and lace up me toes! Now me latest fiancé's turned out to be a proper disappointment. He told me himself—he said he could live on me forever. Then he asked if he could borrow me watch. So I felt sure that meant he was going to pop the question. 'Stead of that he popped me watch! Ah well, it's not the first time I've been looked over and overlooked!

Song 5: Waiting at the Church

(*Singing*)   I'm in a nice bit of trouble I confess,
Somebody with me has had a game,
I should by now be a proud and happy bride,
But I've still got to keep old Twanky's name.
I was proposed to by Charlie Oo-Flung-Dung,
In a very gentlemanly way,
Lent him all me money so that he could buy the home,
And punctually at twelve o'clock that day——

Part I, Scene 2

> There was I—waiting at the church,—waiting at
> the church,—waiting at the church!
> When I found he's left me in the lurch,
> Lor' how it did upset me!
> All at once he sent me round a note,
> Here's the very note,
> This is what he wrote——
> "Can't get away,
> To marry you today,
> My wife won't let me!"

The Stage Manager enters with the words on an easel

Widow Twanky repeats the chorus with the audience

Everyone   There was I—waiting at the church,—
waiting at the church,—waiting at the church!
Etc., etc.

Widow Twanky brings on her shopping basket

Widow Twanky   Right now,—there's me groceries. Really the price of things in the shops these days. I mean—half a lettuce and a bottle of gin and bang goes two bob! And I've just traded in me divi for a necklace. A twenty-one carat necklace they promised me! A twenty-one carat necklace! Look at that! (*She holds up a necklace made of twenty-one carrots*) ... Now, where can I put this where no-one'll pinch it? They've got such charming taking ways around here. I've got an idea! I'll get all you boys and girls to look after it for me. Will you? If you see anyone try to pinch me basket—you shout out—loud as you can—"DON'T TOUCH!!" Will you? Come on, let's have a practice. I'll put it down here and pretend to be someone trying to nick me basket. Here we go! (*Practice, ad lib, with audience, until suitable volume is achieved with "DON'T TOUCH!" Finally...*) Splendid!

Citizen creeps on and makes for the basket

So don't forget now. If you see anyone——
Audience   Don't touch!

Widow Twankey chases the Citizen away

2nd Citizen enters and makes for the basket

The business is repeated

2nd Citizen is chased off by Widow Twankey

Police whistles and chase music is heard

Citizens and Tradesmen return

Two comic policemen, Ping and Pong, rush on from opposite sides of the stage, collide and fall over. Ping points DR and they chase off in that direction

Aladdin, barefoot, runs in UR, crosses the stage diagonally, and exits DL

Ping and Pong run in UR and exit after Aladdin

Aladdin enters UL and runs into the laundry through the door marked "In"

Ping and Pong enter UL and go to the "In" door

About to enter, Pong sees the notice "Leave shoes here" and indicates this to Pong. They both take off their shoes, which they leave beneath the notice

Ping and Pong rush through the door

Aladdin emerges from the door marked "Exit"

Large clouds of steam billow out through the doors and window. Aladdin gathers up Ping and Pong's shoes, then grabs a large box marked "Tacks" from a stall. He empties the (imaginary) tacks in front of the laundry

Aladdin exits DL

Ping and Pong come flying down the chute in a cloud of steam

Ping and Pong's uniforms have shrunk. The sleeves only reach their elbows and the trouser legs are above their knees. They now have tiny helmets on their heads. They get up and stagger on to the "tacks". They hop up and down clutching their feet in agony.

Ping and Pong hop off DR

The crowd of onlookers cheer

Citizen What's going on?
2nd Citizen A chase!
3rd Citizen A merry-go-round!
4th Citizen (*a woman*) With Aladdin in the centre I'll be bound!
Girl You're right, old woman. See! Hip, hip, hooray!
  He's dodged the bobbies, now he comes this way!

All cheer

Aladdin re-appears UL

Girls all gather round Aladdin

Musical intro

All Girls Naughty Aladdin!
4th Citizen Needs a thorough shakin'!
Aladdin What me?—"naughty"? You must be mistaken.

Song 6

During the song the Stage Manager enters with the chorus words on an easel. The audience joins in. Repeat the chorus with Aladdin, the Chorus, and the audience. The Chorus exit

Aladdin Hello! What's Ma's shopping doing down here? (*He approaches the basket . . .*)

Part I, Scene 2 11

Audience Don't touch!!
Widow Twanky enters hauling Wishee-Washee on by his ear...
Widow Twanky Aladdin! Oh, that lazy tiresome rascal!
He never pays attention to his Ma's call.
Aladdin! Oh, Aladdin!! Let me reach him.
To treat his poor old mother thus I'll teach him!
You naughty boy! (*She slaps his hand*)
          You're always in a wrangle.
You know I wanted you to turn the mangle!
Aladdin Oh, blow the mangle, and the laundry too!
Wishee It smells of naught but soap and Reckitt's Blue.
Widow Twanky The night before last you came home yesterday, last night you came home this morning, if you come home tomorrow today, you're not sleeping in this house tonight! (*She weeps*)
My child! My child! My ruin and my joy!
My darling, lazy, good-for-nothing boy!

She blows her nose on her handkerchief

Aladdin Oh, Mother, mother, these endearments stay!
Widow Twanky Where have you been since breakfast time today?
You seem to do just whatsoe'er you like.
Where have you been?
Aladdin Well, I have been on strike!
Widow Twanky On what?
Aladdin On strike!
Widow Twanky Where do you learn such stuff?
Wishee We read about it in the "Tele-gruph"!
Aladdin You grown-ups show the way, it's nothing new.
We kids want to be in the fashion too.
And so *we're* striking!
Widow Twanky   You?
Aladdin ⎫
Wishee ⎭ Yes us!!
Widow Twanky   Good Gracious!
What are we coming to? It's most audacious!
Aladdin Just hear me make my speech, Ma!
Widow Twanky   Not more noise!
Aladdin Just hold your tongue while I address the boys.
Come, let me mount upon some big tea-chest, oh,
And from the top I'll make my manifesto.
Children of Peking! Do you approve my action?
Wishee and the Children in the Audience
Yes!!
Aladdin And does our striking attitude give you satisfaction?
Children Yes!!
Aladdin You know the object of our agitations?
At school we get too many multiplications!

Wishee encourages the children's responses

Children Yes!!
Addition For fewer lessons and more play we seek.
We mean to have six holidays a week!
Children Hooray!!
Aladdin Ice-creams and sweets must be provided free!

To the audience

What say you children? Do you all agree?
Children Yes!!
Widow Twanky What will the Peking School Board Council say?
Aladdin Oh, we don't care! At strikes we mean to play.
Up kids and at 'em! Give it to 'em hot!
I'll show the way, and have the first good shot!
Children Hooray!

Aladdin picks up a basket from which he and all the children help themselves to bags of sweets which they throw out to the audience. Wishee-Washee fetches a huge catapult (say 2 ft high), with which he fires bags of sweets into the dress circle. When the sweets are all used up there is the sound of police whistles off stage

Wishee Listen!
Aladdin Peelers!
Widow Twanky Scarper!

All exit quickly

Ping and Pong enter on a long scooter, which they scoot to C. and park. Pong is wearing large, long boots

Song 7

During the song there is a comedy squad drill routine to the music of the chorus

Black-out at end of the song

Ping Hey! What's going on?
Pong By golly the nights are drawing in!
Ping Lights!!!
Pong Someone put a penny in the slot!
Ping *(calling)* Mr——*(Stage Manager's name)*
Pong We'll have to send for Alec.
Ping Alec?
Pong Alec-Trician!
Ping I don't wish to know that! Ah, Mr——

The Stage Manager enters with a torch

Part I, Scene 2

Stage manager What seems to be the trouble?
Ping The lights have gone out! etc.., etc.
Pong We've had a power cut! etc., etc.

Wishee-washee enters

Wishee Please! Me fix!
Ping You fix?
Wishee Me fix!
Ping How're you going to fix?
Wishee Confucius way. Observe ... (*to audience*) Please, all ladies in audience raise right hand. All little girls. All Mummies—raise right hand ...

Ping, Pong, and the Stage Manager encourage the ladies in the audience to do so ...

Wishee Now all gentlemen—all little boys—all Dads—all gentlemen—raise left hand ...

Ping, Pong and the Stage Manager urge the males in the audience to raise their left hands

All lights come on—including front of house

Pong Magic!
Wishee You see?
Ping Hey, how did you do that?
Wishee Confucius, he say, "Many hands make light work!"

All groan

Wishee-Washee and Stage Manager exit

Stage lights return to pre-black out setting. Front of house lights fade out

Abanazar enters riding Ermintrude the camel

There is a long rubber tube attached at one end to Ermintrude's ear. At the other end is a funnel into which Abanazar blows and speaks

Abanazar All right Ermintrude. You may stop here.
Ping What's that?
Pong Ahhhhhh!

They run away from Ermintrude

It's an upside-down cow! It's a monster!
Ping (*to Abanazar*) Have you a licence for that fearful mammal?
Abanazar It's only Ermintrude, a harmless camel.
Ping You can't park that thing here.
Pong This is a restricted zone.
Ping We'll have to commandeer that apparition in the name of the Emperor.
Abanazar (*dismounting*) Help yourself.

The policemen try to catch Ermintrude. She eludes them. Comic chase. Finally they catch her and hold her fast at either end

Ping (*producing notebook*) Now then, we'll have to have your name and address, mate. Who are you?
Abanazar Why do you wish to know?
Ping I'm arresting this 'ere creature on suspicion.
Abanazar My name is Abanazar, the magician.
In conjuring I'm very great,
My tricks cause much dismay,
For instance I can shoot the Moon

He points a finger at the sky—a sound of shots—a whistle of a falling moon

Or turn night into day.

Lights go off and on

I can summon lightning up,

Flash

The mighty thunder too!

Thunder

Cause anything to multiply!

Snatches a flower from his buttonhole and turns it into a bouquet of flowers

Divide them into two!!

Strikes the centre of Ermintrude with the bouquet. The camel divides into two. The policemen, clinging to either end, fall over, rise, and are chased in circles around the stage

> *They exit in opposite directions pursued by the two separate halves of the camel*

Abanazar Now for this boy Aladdin, who my mission shall fulfil.
I need him very badly, though I wish him naught but ill.
Ah! What is this I see? 'Tis the Shop of Widow Twanky!
This dame I'm told is very bold, and just a trifle cranky.
I'll win her over to my plans, which are of course most shady.
I'll knock upon her door forthwith and interview the lady.
But first a subtle subterfuge to which I'll first subject her.
I will pretend I've come here as the Emp'ror's rent collector!

He puts on a bowler hat and knocks on the door of the Laundry. The window flies open. Widow Twanky appears

Abanazar Rent!!
Widow Twanky Spent!!

She slams the window shut

Abanazar Aha! Insolvent! That's all I wanted to know! (*He knocks again*)

Aladdin opens the door

Aladdin Yes?
Abanazar Aladdin?
Aladdin Who wants him?
Abanazar Is your name Aladdin?
Aladdin It is.
Abanazar Then *I* want you!
(*aside*) This is the youth to execute my plan.
(*aloud*) Fine sort of morning! How d'you do, young man!
Aladdin What's your game?
Abanazar Aladdin, your father's name was——
Aladdin Twanky.
Abanazar Right! And in business he was——
Aladdin A tailor.
Abanazar Right again! You are the boy I seek. Aladdin, I am your father's brother!
Aladdin You?—My Uncle??
Abanazar Of course. Did you never hear your father speak of his long lost brother?
Aladdin Never!
Abanazar Exactly! I am that long lost brother he never spoke of! Tell me, have you not the mark of a gooseberry in the middle of your back?
Aladdin No!
Abanazar (*dramatically*) That proves it! 'Tis he! 'Tis thee! (*He embraces Aladdin*) Nephew!! (*He spots Widow Twanky's basket*) Hello! What's this basket doing down here? Does this belong to——
Audience Don't touch!!

Widow Twanky enters

Widow Twanky Now then! Now then! Who's interfering with me reticule?
Aladdin Mother! I've found a new uncle!
Widow Twanky Too late! We've already pawned everything!
Abanazar Madam, I am your husband's brother.
Widow Twanky Well, I'll go to our house! I don't remember ever seeing you before.
Abanazar No, I've got that sort of face. Once seen never remembered.
Widow Twanky What's your name?
Abanazar (*presenting a card*) Abanazar. Dr Abanazar!
Widow Twanky Doctor!!
Abanazar That's right. I took the hypocritic oath and became a hypocrite.
Aladdin Are you famous?
Abanazar Very.
Widow Twanky What are you famous for?
Abanazar I've invented a well-known cure for which there is no known disease!
Aladdin Are you my uncle or are you a fraud?
Widow Twanky Knowing the family as I do he could be both!
  If only poor old Mustapha were here!
Abanazar Who's Mustapha?
Widow Twanky My husband!

Aladdin And my dad!
Abanazar My brother!
Widow Twanky He no brother ever had!
Abanazar Oh yes he did. I was the youngest child,
A harem-scarem boy and always wild.
I ran away from home when but a youth.
I came back yesterday!
Widow Twanky Is this the truth?
Abanazar I've made my fortune, and come home to share it——
Widow Twanky My brother-in-law you say?
Abanazar Yes, yes! I swear it!
So take me to him straight.
Widow Twanky Oh, sir, be brave!
My husband Mustapha is in his grave!
Abanazar (*dramatically*) What? Musty dead? My grief I cannot smother!
Dead! Dead! And never called me brother!
Where art thou now? Where art thou Musty dear?
Excuse me!—while I wipe away this tear!
Widow Twanky (*to Aladdin*)
The poor man's touched! (*She points to her temple*)
Abanazar Grieve not poor widowed dame.
Your son remains. Aladdin is his name?
Aladdin Indeed, good sir, that is my appelation.
Abanazar (*feeling Aladdin's muscles*)
A-lad-indeed to merit a probation!
At once embrace me!
Aladdin No, I shan't!
Abanazar Boy! I'm your uncle, know you!
Aladdin No you—aren't
Widow Twanky (*drawing Aladdin aside*) Aladdin, don't be rash. If what he says is true
(*whispering*) He's loaded with spondoolicks! (*indicating money with her fingers*)
Aladdin (*crossing to Abanazar*) Why Uncle, is that you?
(*He shakes hands with Abanazar*)
Abanazar He'll have a brilliant future I am sure.
Widow Twanky Fat chance of that, my brother. (*She sniffles*) We're so poor!
Abanazar Nay! Poor no longer! See! I've lots of gold!
'Tis his, if only he'll do as he's told.
Widow Twanky (*nudging Aladdin*) Gold! (*To Abanazar*) Excuse me referring to your affliction but could you oblige me with another peep at your fizzog . . .
Yes! Now I come to scan that mug once more
I know I've seen that mottled map before!
Aladdin Oh, mum! We shall be rich! Oh, uncle! (*He kisses Abanazar's cheek*)
Widow Twanky (*holding out her hand for Abanazar to kiss*) Brother!

Part I, Scene 2

Aladdin No more Chinese take-aways for dinner, Mother!
We'll have real meals now!
Widow Twanky   Yes! We'll show the way
With boiled beef!
Aladdin   And carrots.
Widow Twanky   Ev'ry day!
Dear me! Good news I've not been used to latterly.
I wish I had a little *sal volatile*!
Aladdin Come, Uncle, come! For as you've got the oof,
We welcome you most hearty, neath our roof!

Song 8: Boiled Beef and Carrots

Aladdin	When I was a nipper only six months old,
	My mother and my father too——
	They didn't know what to wean me on,
	They were both in a dreadful stew!!
Widow Twanky	We thought of tripe, we thought of steak,
	Or a little bit of old cod's roe.
	I said pop round to the old cook-shop,
	I know what'll make him grow!
Widow Twanky	Boiled beef and carrots!
Aladdin	Boiled beef and carrots!
Abanazar	That's the stuff for your "Darby Kel",
	Makes you fat, and it keeps you well.
	Don't live like vegetarians
	On food they give to Parrots,
	From morn till night
	Blow out your kite
	On Boiled Beef and Carrots!
Widow Twanky	When I got married to old Mustapha,
	That funny little cove next door,
	We went to Shanghai for the week,
	Then we both toddled home once more.
	His pals all met us in the pub
	Said the fellows to him—

Aladdin ⎫ "What cher Fred!
Abanazar ⎭ What did you have for your honeymoon?"
Widow So just for a lark he said:-

The Stage Manager enters with the words on an easel. They invite the audience to join in

All Boiled Beef and Carrots!
Boiled Beef and Carrots!
Etc., etc.,
Abanazar Now I'm their lodger, I'm an artful cove,
"I'm feeling very queer" I say.

Widow Twanky⎫ (*together*) *Feeling Abanazar's pulse and holding his forehead*
Aladdin   ⎭
   We send for the doctor, he comes round
   And he tells him in bed to stay.
Abanazar "Oh dear!" I say, "I do feel bad!"
Aladdin Says my mother with a fond reply—
Widow Twanky "What would you like for a Pick-me-up?"
Abanazar I jump out of bed and cry—
All Boiled Beef and Carrots!
   Boiled Beef and Carrots!
   Etc., etc.

Repeat chorus

   Widow Twanky, Aladdin, and Abanazar exit

   Fanfare of trumpets. Gong! Enter Vizier With Ping and Pong. Ping Carries a small gong which he strikes. Citizens appear as the Vizier reads from a scroll. Finally Wishee-Washee and Aladdin enter towards the end of the announcement

Vizier Take notice! This being the first day of the moon,
   Also the thirtieth from the last monsoon,
   The fair Princess Badroulbadour today
   To take her bath will come this very way!
   And as no eye on royalty must drop,
   Clear all the streets, and each shut up his shop!
   By order of the mighty King Whang
   Booriboo Ghoola-Hoopla, Black Gang Chang!

   The Vizier exits

Aladdin The fair Princess! At her I'll have a gander!
   They say she's very beautiful,—I wonder!
   This pillar-box will suit my sly intention,
   A very useful British-made invention!

He climbs into the pillar-box, his face appearing at the aperture for letters

Ping Now then you lot! Buzz off, and sling your hook!
   No-one upon the Princess' face may look!

He cracks a whip

Pong Be off!—and take your China mugs away!
   Her Royal Highness comes, so clear the way!

He cracks a whip and hits himself on the ear

   During the following aria the Princess's palanquin is carried on, attended by Swee-Tee and Ainchee-Nice, her "Ladies-in-waiting"

Part I, Scene 2

Song 9: Aria—None Shall Peep

Ping (*or Pong*) None shall peep!
None shall peep!
The Princess' constitution——
'Al walk to her ablution
None may observe, on
Dire pain of retribution——
Swift execution!

Avert your eyes when you're saluting
You must not look when she's ablu-u-ting,——
So, heedful keeping,
And no peeping,
While she's a-bluting
None shall peep!

There'll be no glimpses
While the Princess rinses
Or takes her shower!

Chorus (*covering their eyes as they bow to the palanquin*)
Avert our eyes while we're saluting!
We must not look when she's ablu-u-ting!

They turn and commence to back out, bowing to the palanquin

Ping (*or Pong*) When she's a-soaping,
And the sponge she's groping,
There shall be no snooping,
For that's when none must peep!
None shall peep!
None shall peep!

Ping and Pong exit

The curtain on the princess's Palanquin is drawn back, and the Princess steps out

Gong!

Princess (*over soft musical accompaniment*)
A moment's peace! Oh, thank the stars for this!
To get away from court to me is bliss,
With rank and pride, all boastful with deceit,
And love-sick courtiers always at one's feet,
With silver tongues and venom in their hearts
To me a most unhappy mind imparts.

Ainchee Your Royal Highness should be calm, and try
To put aside these fancies. Now were I
A great Princess, my troubles soon I'd end 'em,
Those courtiers to the right-about I'd send 'em,
And find a youth who'd love me for myself,
Without a craving for my lands and wealth.

Princess 'Tis very strange, but in my dreams at night
I sometimes see a youth with face so bright,

That fills my heart with love, and makes me sad
  To think I'll never find the handsome lad.

Aladdin, in the pillar-box, sneezes! The Princess, Swee-Tee, and Ainchee-Nice are startled

The music stops

Princess What's that? Is anybody looking?
Swee-Tee \
Ainchee / No, not one!
Princess I wish someone *would* look!
Swee-Tee \
Ainchee / (*shocked*) Your Highness!
Princess   Just for fun!
Swee-Tee The Emp'ror grows more Western ev'ry day.
  But still the law stands.
Ainchee   What we need I say
  Is votes for Women!
Swee-Tee   Ainchee, that's insane!
Princess 'Twould not be quite so strange if I were plain.
Swee-Tee But you are pretty. That's why none may peep.
Aladdin (*emerging from the pillar box*)
  A silent tongue no longer can I keep.
  The Emp'ror's foolish edict I'll defy!
  How beautiful she is! . . . Oh my!
  Your Royal Highness! (*He kneels*)

Swee-tee and Ainchee run off

Swee-tee \
Ainchee / (*together, as they go*) Help, help, help! A spy!
          Hear me if you can,
Aladdin My sweet Princess——
Princess (*aside*)   Oh! What a nice young man!
  And such a handsome boy! It's too absurd
  That I can't speak to him one little word!
  (*To Aladdin*)
  You're rather bold to stop me in the street.
Aladdin My only chance your lovely self to meet.
  I know I'm very rash, but love will sure excuse me.
  Sweet Princess, I adore you!
Princess (*aside*)   How beautifully he woos me!
  The hero of my dreams! My heart will not keep steady;
  I must not seem too willing, though I like him so already.
Aladdin (*aside*)
  With all respect and modesty I'd say
  I here behold the future Mrs A!
Princess What would Papa say?! Yet I like the feeling!
  Love is a passion there is no concealing!

Part I, Scene 2

Song 10

During the song the Stage Manager enters with the chorus words on an easel

The Audience joins in the song. Repeat the Chorus, at the end of which Aladdin and the Princess kiss

Ping and Pong enter from opposite directions, together with the Vizier

Vizier What's this? A ruffian looking at the Princess? Seize him and down with him! Kill him, more or less!

The Policemen surround Aladdin and approach him

   Cut his head off!

Ping and Pong take a step forward

Aladdin (*to the Policemen*) Want yours punched?
Vizier   Jump to it!

Aladdin raises his fist. The Policemen do a little jump in the air, and back off a step

Vizier Take him forthwith to prison or you'll rue it!
   Where's the Executioner?
Pong He's probably taking a walk round the block!
Vizier I don't wish to know that!
   Away with him at once!
Princess   This shan't be! I forbid it!
   'Twas out of admiration for me that he did it!
Ping (*gaping*) The Princess!! (*He covers his eyes*)
Pong (*also gaping*) In the flesh! Oooh, what a beauty!

Ping nudges Pong, who hastily covers his eyes

Princess (*to Aladdin*) Fear not, sweet youth!
Aladdin   Sweet heart!
Vizier (*to the policemen*)   Come! Do your duty!
   Seize him immediately, and off to prison drag him.
   And if he dare object then violently scrag him!
Ping Hello! Hello! What's this?
Pong   The Princess!
Ping   Well I'm blessed!
   If she ain't thrown herself across his stalwart chest!
Princess If he's to die——
Ping   She sticks to him like glue!
Princess ——Prepare a coffin large enough for two!
   For by his side I'll die and buried be,
   And o'er the Styx with him I'll ferried be!
Vizier Styx! Fiddlesticks! Men, tear him limb from limb!

Ping You first!
Pong No you!
Princess Stay! You shall *not* harm him!
Vizier (*to the Princess*)
  This conduct's most outrageous. Think, madam, who you are!
Princess Don't care! I'll do as *I* like!
Vizier I shall tell your pa!
  If his displeasure you'd not seek to earn
  You quickly to the Palace will return.
  (*to Swee-Tee and Ainchee*)
  Ladies convey her. (*to the Princess*) No pleadings can avail!
  And cast that rascal Twanky into gaol!
Princess Why would you shut me off from earthly joy?
  I love this youthful, handsome Chinese boy!
Vizier Shocking!
Ping Scandalous!
Pong She's got a point, I must say!

Ping hits Pong

Princess Release my sweetheart instantly!
Vizier Take him away!

Policemen seize Aladdin, and put him in chains

  Abanazar enters

Abanazar Aladdin seized? 'Tis time I interfered,
  Or all my plans are likely to be queered.
Aladdin Oh, Uncle! Uncle! Tell me what to do!
Abanazar Trust Abanazar, boy. I'll pull you through.
  Sirs! Why do you this stripling thus assail?
Ping He broke the law. He's got to go to gaol.

Song 11

Ping We've got to run him in,
 We're p'licemen!
Princess
Swee-Tee } Oh, please don't run him in,
Ainchee Mr P'liceman!
Swee-Tee } He's his mother's only joy.
Ainchee
Princess And he's such a darling boy!
Princess
Swee-Tee } So *please* don't run him in,
Ainchee Mr P'liceman!
Ping } Oh, we've got to run him in.
Pong } We're P'licemen.

Princess ⎫ Oh, please don't run him in,
Swee-Tee ⎬ Mr P'liceman!
Ainchee ⎭
Ping ⎱ We don't wish to cause a fuss,
Pong ⎰ *(taking hold of Aladdin)*
    So just come along of us!
    'Cos we've got to run you in,
    We're P'licemen!

They start to lead Aladdin away

Ping Come!
Abanazar Abracadabra, Abracadee!
    Lapsang Suchong, and Earl Grey's Tea!

He makes a magic sign. Flash! Everyone freezes except Aladdin

Abanazar Fear not Aladdin, they're within my power,
    But we must leave Peking within the hour.
Aladdin Abandon the Princess? No, Uncle, no!
Abanazar Into the country we must quickly go.
Aladdin I cannot leave her. Here let me remain.
    I long to kiss my Princess once again.
Abanazar Boy, this is folly. You deserve a whipping!
Aladdin I care not! Life without her's not worth living!

He takes the Princess's hand

Abanazar You yearn for her, boy?
Aladdin   Do I, Do I not!!
    With hopeless love this bosom's burning hot!
Abanazar But why say "hopeless"?
Aladdin   It must ever be.
    Can one so high look down on such as me?
Abanazar Quite so! You've hit the truth, Aladdin, which is
    No man has any chance here without riches.
    Boy, be advised. *First* seek for wealth and fame,
    And *then* return, the Princess' hand to claim.
    I'll make your fortune!
Aladdin   How can that be so?
Abanazar Not far from here a magic cave I know.
    It's full of gold and precious jewels rare.
Aladdin Gold?
Abanazar Riches in abundance!—if you care
    To enter it, which easily you can.
Aladdin Then say no more, dear Uncle. I'm your man!

    (He approaches the Princess)

Aladdin I'll buy her bonnets, jewels, gorgeous dresses,
    A golden brush and comb for her fine tresses.
Abanazar Think of that wealth, and of your Princess fair!

Aladdin To gain her hand all dangers I would dare!

Abanazar leads Aladdin away from the Princess

Abanazar Leave now your sweetheart. Let's be on our way.
For we must reach the cave by break of day.

Aladdin exits

(*Aside*)
Then for the magic lantern we can search,
And that once found, I'll leave him—in the lurch!!
Ah—ha! ha! ha! ha! ha!

Abanazar exits

Music

Wishee-Washee enters with his catapult

He sees the frozen group. He approaches the Policemen and the Vizier, discovers their frozen state, and then sets about re-arranging them. He pulls one of Ping's legs back, and bends it upwards in a preparative kicking position aimed at Pong's bottom. He raises Pong's arm holding a truncheon over the Vizier's head. He retreats to the side of the stage and fires his catapult at Ping's bottom, whose leg flies through and up to kick Pong's bottom, whose truncheon comes down on the Vizier's head. They all wake up and unfreeze. The Vizier clutches his head, turns, espies the truncheon in Pong's hand, and chases Ping and Pong in a circle

Ping, Pong and the Vizier chase off

Black-out

Scene 3

Outside the magic cave (frontcloth)

A waterfall is painted on the cloth to one side of the (practical) cave entrance. The latter is blocked by a huge boulder

Ermintrude enters, loaded with a travelling pack, followed by Aladdin

Aladdin Hi! Ermintrude! Not so fast! Wait for me! You've left Uncle Abanazar half-way up the mountain.

Ermintrude stamps her foot angrily

What's the matter? Don't you like Uncle?

Ermintrude shakes her head and trembles at the knees

Does he frighten you?

Ermintrude nods

Well, don't worry, I won't let him hurt you.

Ermintrude snuggles her head onto Aladdin's shoulder

Part I, Scene 3

Oh, that's all right, don't mention it! Anyway, he won't be here for a bit. He's completely out of puff. It's very exhausting climbing mountains.

Ermintrude shakes her head and gestures with her foreleg that there's nothing to it

Oh, you don't think so?

Ermintrude shakes her head

Well, it's all right for you. You've got four legs. We've only got two.

Ermintrude dances a few steps, showing off her legs

Oh, yes, very elegant! You ought to go on the stage.

Ermintrude whispers in Aladdin's ear

You've been on the stage?

Ermintrude nods and whispers

You played the leading part? What in?

Ermintrude whispers

The Lady of the *Camel*ias! I don't wish to know that! Do you do much dancing?

Ermintrude nods

Will you dance for us now?

Ermintrude nods

... What are you waiting for?

Ermintrude cocks one ear

Music?

Ermintrude nods

What music would you like?

Ermintrude whispers

Hansel and Gretel? That's a bit posh isn't it? Why Hansel and Gretel?

Ermintrude whispers

Because it's by Humperdinck!! I don't wish to know that either! you'll have to make do with what we've got. (*To the orchestra*) Maestro, please.

Music 11a

Ermintrude dances with Aladdin to the air of "The Elephants" from "The Carnival of the Animals" by Saint Saens

Abanazar, holding his staff, enters at the end of the dance

Abanazar So! Here you are!

Ermintrude double-takes and gallops off

Aladdin   Wait! Ermintrude!
Abanazar   Don't worry.
  She knows she can't escape me in a hurry.
  I've cast a spell on her. She cannot run.
  Well! well! It seems our journey's nearly done,
  We've walked and ridden, I think, far enough.
Aladdin So, let's turn back again!
Abanazar   Turn back? Pshaw! Stuff!
Aladdin This place looks gloomy!
Abanazar (*aside*)   Better will it fit
  My purpose! (*Aloud*) Come! Let's rest ourselves a bit.
Aladdin Would I were home again! Dear me!
  Please, Uncle, I think Mother's waiting tea!

Aladdin makes to go, but is pulled back by Abanazar

  My poor old mum you made me leave behind.
Abanazar You've come to make your fortune bear in mind.
  We want no meddling "mums" to interfere.
  You'll do as you are told. Is that quite *clear*!!?
Aladdin (*aside*)
  I fear some trickery, some evil plan.
  Well then, I'd better face him like a man.

(*to Abanazar*)

  Look, you can't bully me, so please don't try.
  If you doubt that just look me in the eye!
  Your manner stern don't frighten *me* at all,
  If you wish to address me (*he shouts*) please don't bawl!!
Abanazar Tut, tut, dear boy, you're quite mistaken, really,
  To tell the truth I love you very dearly,
  My temper's rather quick, I must confess,
  I merely state the facts, no more, no less.
  Examine for yourself this piece of gold.
  Now if you're enterprising, brave, and bold,
  I soon can show you where there's stocks of it!
Aladdin Stocks?
Abanazar In blocks! Huge, great enormous rocks of it!
Aladdin But *how* can I get gold? Where is this pelf?
Abanazar Beneath your feet!! You've but to help yourself!
(*He points to the rock*)
  Behold the entrance! Here below us lies a cave
  Of wealth enough to make a Croesus rave.
Aladdin But how does one get in?
Abanazar I'll show you quick,
  A simple spell I know will do the trick.
  But 'ere I work this fearful incantation
  I rather think there's too much 'lumination.

Part I, Scene 3

(*To the lighting box*)
    Just douse the glim, and as it's Pantomime
    Oblige us kindly with a bright green lime!

The Lights turn green

    Ah, that's the style! And don't forget the thunder!

There is a distant rumble of thunder as Abanazar draws a magic circle with his staff, then falls on one knee, and raises his arms heavenwards, as he chants his incantation

Aladdin (*during the above*)
    What on earth's he doing now I wonder?

The roll of a drum

Abanazar Sprites of evil! Gnomes of noisome sin!
    Imps of forked flaming tongues your fiendish toil begin!
    Blast with your breath an opening to the cave,
    (*aside*)
    And sweep *him* swiftly to his living grave!
    Abracadabra! Abracadee!
    Open thy portals, oh Cavern, for me.
    Hark to my password—the magical key!——
    It's "Open..."!... It's "Open..."!... "*Open*..."
    Ye Gods!! I've forgotten!... "*Open*..."

The audience will whisper it

Aladdin They know it!
    (*To the audience*) What is it? Tell it to *me*!
    "Open...?" "Open...?"
Audience   Sesame!
Aladdin   Open *what*??
Audience   Sesame!!

Lightning. Thunder. The entrance to the cave rolls open. Aladdin approaches the entrance

Aladdin What sights, what wonders shall I now behold?
Abanazar (*aside*) You'll be surprised!
    (*aloud*)   First, do as you are told!
    Go! Tell me what you see!
Aladdin (*peering in*)   Bright, shining things.
Abanazar What else?
Aladdin   Great heaps of golden rings!
    Diamonds!—beyond a hundred misers' dreams!
    Why here's enough for ten Welsh water-schemes!
Abanazar But is that all? Be quick you foolish scamp!
Aladdin I see... I see...
Abanazar   Yes? Yes?
Aladdin   I see a lamp!

Abanazar (*aside*)
　At last! At last the wond'rous lamp is mine!——
　Wealth power, and all it doth combine!
　Upon the pinnacle of fame I stand,
　The lives and fates of millions in my hand!
(*to Aladdin*)
　That lamp is mine! Go down and bring it here!
Aladdin　I'm frightened!
Abanazar　Foolish whelp! There's naught to fear.

Abanazar and Aladdin sing

Song 12: Down With You Quickly

Abanazar	To the cavern down below
	You must very quickly go!
Aladdin	Oh, I'd rather not, I fear that *I* shall fall!
Abanazar	You must enter straight away!
	If you dare to say me nay
	Then just bid goodbye to mother, home and all!
Aladdin	Oh, I'll go home and tell my Ma
	What a naughty man you are!
Abanazar	Then it may be that you'll never see her more!
Aladdin	I shall holler, don't you know,
	Now won't you let a fellow go?
Abanazar	No, down at once! I'll show you to the door.
	Down with you quickly, if you mean to go at all,
	Or I'll settle soon your hash,
	You'll go down with such a smash
	That your ribs and nose,
	Your thumbs and toes,
	Will suffer in the fall!
	Down! or the Cavern will close!

　　　(*Repeat chorus*)

Finally, Abanazar draws Aladdin to the cave entrance and pushes him in

Abanazar (*raising his arms in triumph*)
　Ha! ha! The Magic Lamp will soon be mine,
　And with it won't this Wizard cut a shine!

Thunder

　The storm witch and her winds speed through the air,
　And as the fairies dance, let all beware!!!
　Ah, ha! ha! ha! ha! ha!

Lightning

Black-out

Scene 4

Inside the magic cave

A small dragon's head stands on a ledge. In its open mouth is the Magic Lamp

Music 12a: Dance of the Spiders (music: Le Rouet d'Omphale by Saint Saens)

This is a ballet for model spiders which descend on the end of spiders' webs from above, and two pairs of dancers in eight-legged costumes

The dancers exit at the end of the dance

Aladdin enters the cave through a small hole high up

Aladdin Oh Uncle, it's very dark down here!
Echo Down here!

Abanazar's head appears in the hole high up

Abanazar Descend!
Echo Descend!
Abanazar Descend!
Echo Descend!
Abanazar Descend, and lose no time!
Echo Lose no time! no time! no time! no time!
Aladdin Oh!! Uncle!
Abanazar What's the matter?
Aladdin It's so deep!
Abanazar So what? Do you have vertigo?
Aladdin About eighty feet if I fall down there! ... *Ohh!*
Abanazar Now, what is it?
Aladdin I thought I saw a huge black beetle!
Abanazar Never mind the beetles, find the lamp!
Aladdin *Oh!*
Abanazar What is it *now*?
Aladdin I saw a rat!
Abanazar Wretch!! Do my bidding!
Aladdin —Well, I will endeavour.
Abanazar Or be immured in that dark cave forever.
 Quickly descend!
Echo Descend! Descend! Descend! Descend!

Lights come up on the chests of gold and precious stones, and on the rest of the cave with jewel-bedecked trees

Aladdin Oh dear! I say! Oh my!
Abanazar What do you see, my sweet, observant boy?
Aladdin The cavern sparkles, radiant as the sun,
 With gold and jewels by the hundred ton.

Close on each side as far as eye can reach
Hang priceless gems, all worth a fortune each!
Abanazar The lamp! The lamp!
Aladdin The diamond laden trees
Flash forth their myriad stars to curtsey in the breeze!
Abanazar Just throw your active clacker out of gear,
And get that lamp this instant, do you hear?
Aladdin I hear, Uncle, but I *must* take a bit of gold home for Mother!
Abanazar Mother Schmother! Hurry up!
Aladdin I'm doing my best! . . . Uncle!
Abanazar What is it?
Aladdin I can see it!
Abanazar What?
Aladdin The lamp!!
Abanazar Seize it immediately!
Aladdin But it's inside a dragon's mouth!
Abanazar Never mind! Get it! Get it!

Aladdin climbs up and puts forward his hand to take the lamp. As he does so a puff of smoke and fire issue from the mouth of the dragon's head, accompanied by a roar

Aladdin Oh, Uncle! Uncle! The dragon vomits fire!
Abanazar Fool! Use your hand with the Magic Ring! It will protect you. Get the lamp!

Aladdin does so

Chorus of Echoes Aladdin! Aladdin! Be wary and wise!
Though rubies and diamonds gladden your eyes,
Take the lamp quickly, and with it ne'er part,
And then shall be granted the wish of your heart!
Aladdin I've got it, Uncle!
Abanazar At last! Now! Quick! Hand it to me!
Aladdin I want to have a look round first, Uncle. Hello! More gold and jewels!
Abanazar You have to give me the lamp of your own free will, or its power to me is useless. Come on now! Pass it out to me!
Aladdin Oh, all right then, Uncle. But first give me a hand up. I can't get out otherwise.
Abanazar No, you give me the lamp first. I'll help you out afterwards.
Aladdin I don't like the sound of that. I don't know if I can trust him. Why does he want me to give him the lamp first? Shall I give it to him? (*To the audience*) What do you say, children? Shall I give him the lamp first?
Audience No!
Aladdin Don't you think I should trust him?
Audience No!!
Abanazar What's all that noise? Just hand me up the lamp! Your hash I'll quickly settle, saucy scamp!

Aladdin No thank you, Uncle dear, I'm not so dense!
You help me out first. That makes much more sense!
Abanazar Impertinence! Give me the lamp I say!
Aladdin As long as I'm in here the lamp shall stay!
Abanazar It's mine! Such impudence I never saw!
Aladdin Possession, sir, is nine tenths of the law!
Abanazar The lamp! Give me the lamp!
Aladdin   First help me out!
Your good intentions I begin to doubt.
Abanazar You refuse?
Aladdin   Yes!
Abanazar   Then, to a living tomb
I shall consign you till the crack of doom!
You'll lie unheeded,—by the world forgot.
Amidst your riches you will slowly rot!
Aladdin No! (*He tries to climb out of the hole*)
Abanazar (*pushing him back*)
By the furies I will circumvent you.
Down! Down to Purgat'ry, and say I sent you!
Aladdin Uncle!
Abanazar   The lamp!
Aladdin   No!
Abanazar   Then accept your fate!
Your doom is sealed! (*He makes a magic sign*)
Aladdin   Wait, Uncle, wait!
Abanazar   Too late!

Crack of thunder. The rock rolls over, and the entrance is sealed

Aladdin Gone!! Left me here amidst the gathering gloom
Of this vast cave, predestined for my tomb.
Come back! (*He beats against the rock*)
Come back!! Don't shut me from the sky!
Uncle! Take the lamp! Don't leave me here to die!

Laughter outside the cave. Echoes of laughing voices within

Aladdin The mocking echoes turn my piteous prayer
To scornful laughter, hastening my despair!
Oh, Mother! Help me please! At any cost!
That's foolish! She can't hear me now. I'm lost!
Home, love, and life I've forfeited forever,——
My end is nigh,—which death's cold hand shall sever.

Hissing noise from above. A large spider descends to just above and behind Aladdin

Aladdin What was that? I feel as if something were watching me. I daren't look! (*To the Audience*) Is there anything there? ... What is it? ... Where is it? ... Behind me?

The spider ascends

... Where? ... There's nothing there! You're pulling my leg.

The spider descends elsewhere

... What? ... Where? ... Over here? ... Where then? ... Over there?

The spider ascends

There's nothing there. You're making it up. (*Ad lib*) I know what to do. Let's get rid of all these cobwebs once and for all. I want you to help me. When I say "Go" I want all of you to wave your hands about, high over your heads, and go like this—(*he blows a raspberry*). And that'll knock all the cobwebs down and frighten the spiders away. Are you ready? After three!

As he counts the spiders appear again

One—two—three! Go!!

The Audience wave their hands. Streamers are thrown over the Audience's heads. The spiders disappear

Ah, that's better! That's cleared them away. But what's to happen to me? And what will happen to my Princess?
Oh, Sweet Princess, engraven on my heart,
It chills my soul to think that I must part
With your sweet self. If but my thoughts could bring her.
Hello, what's this? The ring upon my finger!
I quite forgot! It's magic I believe!
How dull it is. I'll rub it on my sleeve!

Aladdin rubs the ring. Flash!

The Geni of the ring appears

Geni What is your will? You've but to ask and I
To execute your ev'ry wish shall try.
Aladdin What—*any*thing I ask?
Geni   Aye, anything!
Aladdin Who are you, pray?
Geni   The Geni of the Ring!
Whoever on his finger wears that band
Owns me as slave to order and command.
Aladdin Can you from out this cave then set me free?
Geni I can and will, if you will follow me.
Where would you go?
Aladdin   Peking!
Geni   My Magic Power
Shall whisk you there in less than half an hour!
Where is the lamp?
Aladdin   There lies the hideous thing,
The cause of all my woes ...

Part I, Scene 4

Geni Great joy it yet shall bring!
(*Taking up the lamp*)
This lamp is sacred and its power divine.
While thine it is, then all the world is thine.
Keep thou the lamp. It was of old
In ages past, by many a sage foretold
That you would win it, and that it would bring
To you a fair Princess and wedding ring!
Aladdin Badroulbadour! My love!
Geni Within a day
She shall be yours!
Aladdin Oh happiness!
Geni Yet stay!
This lamp is now committed to your keeping,
Jealously guard it, waking, aye, and sleeping!

Aladdin takes the lamp from the Geni

My lord commands! I am his slave this day.
Thine is the power—to hear is to obey!
Thou wouldst be gone from hence with lightning speed——
To home, and love, and happiness! . . . Proceed!!

Fiery Spirits enter

Music 13 "Danse Macabre"

Dance of the fiery spirits. To the main theme they sing

Spirits Aladdin! Aladdin!
     Your task is done.
The ring is gained
     The lamp is won.
Now you may rove
     Over earth and sea!
Hail to Aladdin!
     You're free! You're free!

The Geni makes a magic sign. Thunder. The back wall of the cave splits in two to reveal a bright blue sky and brilliant daylight shining on a sparkling waterfall

A vertical, endless, diarama-roll representing cascading water, which is turned continuously

As if in a vision appears the image of Princess Badroulbadour. High in the sky hangs the effigy of Queen Victoria. Aladdin kneels and bows his head, then rises and walks towards the light

CURTAIN

PART II

Scene 5

Widow Twanky's Laundry (Interior)

An elaborate, steam-driven washing machine, with a tangle of pipes (mostly painted on backcloth—except for practical parts)—all worked by a huge lever. A window R, *an entrance upstage, and a twisting panel in the upper wall*

A large skip or clothes-basket RC, *a table, an ironing board, and a huge mangle* L

Opening chorus for laundry-girls and boys:

Song 14: The Chinese Laundrymen

All Ching, ching, Chinamen
We're the clothes refinermen,
Hang 'em on the lina-men,
In the Chinese Laundry!
Ching, ching, Chinamen,
We're the clothes refinermen,
Hang 'em on the lina-men,
In the Chinese Laundry!

Laundry Worker Don't think we're a Peking atrocity,
2nd Laund We don't bear you any animosity.
3rd Laund "Twanky's" take in washing and——
4th Laund Trade just now is not so very grand!
1st Laund There's Chinese laundries everywhere,
  They take our biz away!
2nd Laund And since we are all Chinese too
  We scrub away all day!
All Ching, ching, Chinamen,
  We're the clothes refinermen,
    Etc., etc.
(*Repeat chorus*)

A factory hooter sounds

All Lunch break!

Everyone cheers

  Wishee-Washee enters with a large soup tureen and several ladles

Part II, Scene 5

The laundry workers take up the ladles, sip the contents of the tureen and spit it out in unison. Wishee-Washee digs down deep into the tureen with his ladle, and pulls out a pair of overalls

Song 15: Who Threw the Overalls in Widow Twanky's Chowder?

Wishee	'Ere!
	Widow Twanky made this chowder
	Just about an hour ago.
	Everything went in that should
	The Widow, she's not slow.
	You're treated here like gentlefolk—
All	We try to act the same!
Wishee	And only for what's happened, well,
	It is an awful shame!
Laundry Worker	When Wishee-Washee dished the chowder out,
	A big surprise we got!
2nd Laund	He's found this pair of overalls
	At the bottom of the pot
Wishee	The Widow, she'll go ripping mad,
	Her eyes all bulging out,
	She'll jump upon the Pi-a-no!
	And loudly she will shout——
Wishee	Who threw the overalls
	In Widow Twanky's Chowder?
	Nobody speaks!
	So I'll shout it all the louder!
	It's a dirty trick, that's true,
	And we'll lick whoever threw
	The Overall in Widow Twanky's Chowder!
All	Who threw the overalls
	In Widow Twanky's Chowder?
	Etc., etc.
Wishee	I've dragged the pants from out our soup
	And laid 'em on the floor.
All	We all swear upon our lives
	We've not seen them before!
1st Laund	They've been plastered up with mortar!
2nd Laund	And they're worn out at the knee!
All	They've had their many ups and downs
	As we can plainly see!
Wishee	Well, when Widow Twanky she comes to
	She'll start to cry and pout,
	She's had them in the wash today
	And forgot to take them out.
	And really there is no excuse
	For what's been done tonight,
	So let's put music to the words,

                    And sing with all our might!——
All   Who threw the overalls
                    In Widow Twanky's Chowder?
                    Etc., etc.

All repeat the chorus

The factory hooter sounds

Wishee End of lunch break! And I'm still famished. Here, let's see what's in this basket!

The Audience call out "Don't touch"

Widow Twanky enters, dressed in her laundering outfit

Widow Twanky Come along! Come along! Back to work you lot! It's time to do the Emperor's laundry. They'll be calling for it any minute now! (*She opens the huge clothes-basket and takes out a list*) Let's see what we've got here. Thirty-eight knickers! (*She holds up a pair with one leg*) Ooh! Look here! Larceny! Someone's stolen half a nicker!

Widow Twanky and Washee toss the various articles of clothing into the copper of the washing-machine

"Twenty-seven vests!" (*She holds up a vest full of holes*) Ah, that'll be the vicar's vest!
Wishee How do you know that's the vicar's vest?
Widow Twanky "Holey, holey, holey!"

They toss the vests into the copper

"Eighteen pairs of socks."
Wishee (*pulling out brightly coloured socks*) Ah! the Emperor's Golfing Socks!
Widow Twanky Golfing socks?
Wishee (*pushing his fist through the heel*) He's got a hole in one!
Widow Twanky Here's a pair of combs. Now look at that! Typical! No name in them and all the buttons missing! Unidentified flyless objects! (*She throws them into the copper and pulls out a pair of bloomers*) Now this one's got the right idea. She's got her name printed on the inside ...Harrods! (*or local store extant in 1890s*). (*She throws them into the copper*) Good for you, Harrod! ... That the lot?
Wishee That's it!
Widow Twanky Start the machine!

Music from Song 15 is reprised during laundry business

Wishee-Washee pulls over the huge lever. There is much steam and a terrible banging noise

Hold it! Hold it! It's bunged up again. Fetch the push-me-pull-me!

Wishee-Washee exits and returns with a very long chimney-sweep's brush which he can barely control. The brush swings out over the audience, etc.

Eventually Widow Twanky succeeds in pushing the brush-head into the top of the machine. Wishee-Washee gives a push on the handle, which disappears into the machine, as also does he, up to his waist, leaving his legs waving in the air. The brush-head shoots out through a separate pipe coming out of the wall to between Widow Twanky's legs. (NB separate brush-heads worked independently). She leaps into the air

Pull it out! Pull it out!

Wishee-Washee pulls the brush out of the machine—the brush-head disappears from on stage, and then reappears again at the end of the handle from out of the machine. It has several fish and a dead cat hanging from it. Again Wishee-Washee can hardly control it, and it swings out over the audience as he returns it to offstage. As he does so Widow Twanky closes the machine lid and pulls the lever. Again there is much steam and a sound like the engine of a liner as the machine goes into operation

Widow Twanky brings the ironing-board to C. *From the large skip she takes a pair of combs and places them over the ironing-board. Wishee-Washee returns with a huge iron, which together they place on the ironing-board. The ironing-board sinks to the floor. (NB it has wheels on the end of its crossed legs, the bottom halves of which are joined together by springs, so that when pressure is released the ironing-board stands up again on its own)*

Widow Twanky irons two or three items on the board which springs up and down as she does so. The machine gives a whistle

Wishee It's done!
Widow Twanky Right! Get 'em out and we'll put 'em through the mangle!

They take out the clothes from the machine. The bloomers have shrunk and are tiny. The combs are as stiff as a board with outstretched arms and legs like a crucified figure

Wishee Ooh! May I have the pleasure? (*He waltzes round the room with the combs as a partner*)
Widow Twanky (*crossing to mangle*) Never mind that. Come on, let's get on with the mangling!

The mangle has been set up DS, *with the turning wheel* US, *and the far side of the rollers out of view of the audience, and facing into the wings. The top roller moves up and down easily to admit articles of any size*

Wishee-Washee picks up the articles and puts them into the rollers as Widow Twanky turns the wheel. The third article (combs?) gets stuck

(*Turning the handle*) Give it a shove!

Wishee-Washee retreats a few steps, then takes a run at the mangle, trips over his own foot, and goes hands first into the rollers. He disappears through the rollers. Widow Twanky reverses the turning wheel and a flattened "cut out" effigy of Wishee-Washee returns through the roller, and falls at her feet on the floor. She places the "cut out" into the washing-machine and pulls the lever. Steam! Clanking engines. She pushes the lever back, opens the lid of the machine, and Wishee-Washee steps out, whole again

Widow Twanky Now stop playing the fool, and give us a hand!

Ping and Pong enter, whistles blowing

Ping Is anyone at home?
Wishee Now what's to do?
Pong Ah! There she is!
Widow Twanky Beg 'pardon? Who are you? And what do you want here?
Ping Well, if it please yer, Or if it don't, — we've come to make a seizure!
Widow Twanky It's the Bum Bailiffs! It's the Bum Bailiffs! Oh, sirs! Have pity on a poor, lone woman!
Ping It's not our fault you're a lone woman!
Widow Twanky Then why can't you leave a lone woman alone?
Wishee Ma!
Widow Twanky Yes?
Wishee Tell me something.
Widow Twanky Yes?
Wishee Why do you call them *Bum* Bailiffs?
Widow Twanky Because they're always after people who get behind in their rent!

Ping whistles and points at the furniture

No, not my furniture!
Ping Quick! Seize that table!
Widow Twanky Oh, you won't take it all!
Ping Yes, all we're able!

Ping prepares to take the ironing board. Wishee-Washee picks up the iron

Widow Twanky Leave that! It is my livelihood, you know.
Ping No, not one stick. We mean to have the lot.

Widow Twanky takes the iron from Wishee-Washee

Widow Twanky Then better take this first while it is hot!

Widow Twanky drops the iron on Ping's foot. Ping and Pong blow their whistles. Flashing lights. A comic chase ensues (NB a double of Widow Twanky is added for the chase, referred to below as Widow Twanky B)

Wishee dives into the skip and pulls the lid down

Widow Twanky A runs out of the entrance US pursued by Ping

Pong cautiously approaches the skip

Widow Twanky B runs in through the panel US, crosses the stage and jumps out of the window

Pong leaps out of the window after Widow Twanky B

Part II, Scene 5

> Widow Twanky A enters immediately through the panel, again followed by Ping. She exits via the door entrance pursued by Ping
>
> Widow Twanky B appears immediately through the panel, again pursued by Pong and exits via the door
>
> Ping enters through the panel US, unable to see Widow Twanky at all
>
> Pong comes in through the same panel
>
> Ping exits and enters through the panel, still searching
>
> Pong does the same
>
> Each time the panel turns we see Widow Twanky A standing on a ledge on the back of the panel going round and round
>
> Widow Twanky staggers off the panel and across the stage. When she reaches the window Ping and Pong spot her and blow their whistles
>
> Widow Twanky leaps out of the window, followed by Ping and Pong
>
>> Widow Twanky B enters via the panel and climbs into the washing machine
>>
>> Ping arrives just in time to see her and climbs into the washing machine after her
>>
>> Pong arrives in time to see Ping and follows him into the washing machine
>>
>> Widow Twanky A enters through the window to behind Pong

When Pong is safely in the machine Widow Twanky A closes the lid and pulls the lever to start the machine. There is a terrible grinding noise and explosion. Lights stop flickering. Wishee-Washee emerges from the skip. Ping and Pong emerge from the machine. Their uniforms and helmets are shrunken again as in the opening scene

Ping ⎫
Pong ⎭ (*together*) Oh no! Not again!!

They collapse onto each other and stagger about the stage. Wishee-Washee guides them one by one into the mangle, while Widow Twanky turns the handle and winds them through. She then reverses the turning of the wheel, and two "cut-out" cardboard effigies of Ping and Pong emerge from the mangle. Wishee-Washee tosses them out of the window. Then——

Widow Twanky (*dramatically*) Oh woe! Oh woe!
 Why did my boy Aladdin vainly roam?
 They've killed my son, and broken up me home!
 Was ever widow left in such a fix?
 My trade's all gone, and now they want me sticks!
Wishee Cheer up Mother, don't be sad. Although I must admit
 I never liked our uncle's ways,—no not a little bit!—
 Aladdin's safe, I'll bet a bob, and soon will make his way
 Back to his home, and tell us all his doings of the day!

Widow Twanky I can't cheer up! I can't forget, however much I'm trying,
The thought my boy has come to harm is sure to set me crying——

Widow Twanky and Wishee-Washee weep on each other's shoulders. They are joined by two or three laundry workers to sing in close harmony

Song 16: Where Is My Wandering Boy Tonight?

Widow Twanky	Where is my wand'ring boy tonight?—
	The boy of my tenderest care,
	The boy that was once my joy and light,
	The child of my love and prayer?
All	Oh where is my (her) boy tonight?
	Oh where is my (her) boy tonight?
	My (her) heart o'erflows
	For I (she) love(s) him he knows;
	Oh where is my (her) boy tonight?
Wishee	Once he was pure as morning dew,
	As he knelt at his mother's knee;
	No face was so bright, no heart more true,
	And none was so sweet as he.
All	Oh where is my (her) boy tonight?
	Etc., etc.
Laundry workers	Oh could she see her darling boy,
	As fair as in olden time,
	When prattle and smile made home a joy
	And life was a merry chime!
All	Oh where is my (her) boy tonight?
	Etc., etc.
Widow Twanky	Go for my wand'ring boy tonight!
	Go search for him where you will!
	But bring him to me with all his blight,
	And tell him I love him still!
All	Oh where is my (her) boy tonight? Etc., etc.

Aladdin enters on the last lines of the song, and poses with the others in a final tableau. With a wink to the audience, he creeps towards the basket

The Audience shout out

Widow Twanky Aladdin!
Aladdin Mother! Safe I stand before you!
  No thanks for that to Uncle I assure you!
Widow Twanky How could you thus my peace of mind destroy,
  You lazy, tiresome, dear delightful boy!?

Embracing Aladdin

  My ducky, darling, popsy-wopsy pet!

She clouts him

Part II, Scene 5

Where have you been to?!
Widow Twanky advances on the retreating Aladdin
Aladdin I can't tell you yet!
Widow Twanky Where is your uncle?
Aladdin Uncle he is none!
Wishee Ah!!
Widow Twanky Tell me all about it. What's he done?
Aladdin He is a vile and devilish magician!
Wishee I always looked upon him with suspicion!
  I knew he weren't your uncle!
Widow Twanky Oooh! The villain!
  To see him on the tread-mill I'd be willin'!
Aladdin (*to Audience*)
  Such men as he deserve, the mill far more
  Than many a poor man, who with hunger at the door
  Takes a loaf of bread his family to feed,
  And only steals because he's forced by need!
Widow Twanky (*likewise*)
  Your words are true, and Justice, though she's blind
  Might sometimes be with Mercy tempered kind!
Wishee What did he do?
Aladdin Left me to die!
Wishee No he never, that was yesterdie!
Widow Twanky The thief!
Aladdin But then a Geni came to my relief.
Widow Twanky A what?
Aladdin A sort of...fairy!
Wishee A sort of *what*ee?
Widow Twanky God Save the Queen! I think the boy's gone potty!
Aladdin It's true, Mama!
Wishee A fairy!
Aladdin Yes! The sweetest I have known!
Widow Twanky Well, boys like you had better leave the fairies quite alone!
Aladdin I'm hungry, Ma!
Widow Twanky Alas! Like Mother Hubbard,
  I am afraid there's nothing in the cupboard!
Wishee Aladdin! What's that there?
Aladdin It's just a lamp!
  Old Uncle badly wanted it, the scamp!
Wishee Old Uncle! That's a happy thought, my friend!
(*He takes the lamp from Aladdin*)
  We know *another* "uncle" who might lend
  A bob or two on this!
Widow Twanky (*taking the lamp from Wishee*) He will, I trust.
  But first I'll polish off the rust!
Aladdin (*patting his tummy*)
  I couldn't sleep, Ma, dreaming of your grub!

Widow Twanky (*rubbing the lamp with her apron*)
  To sleep perchance to dream, aye, there's the rub!

Flash! Geni of the Lamp appears

Wishee Great Scotland Yard! What is it?
Geni   Have no fear!
Widow Twanky It's the young man for the empties!
Wishee   Oh! What cheer!
Geni (*bowing to the ground*)
  Aladdin! Master! I'm your slave! In me
  The Geni of that Magic Lamp you see.
  Its owner over me holds potent sway.
  Command me!—and your summons I obey!
Widow Twanky Oh, no! Not *another* summons!!
Geni (*to Widow Twanky*)
  From the earth's bowels I have flown to greet you!
Widow Twanky "Well, when you've got to go you've got to go!"
  (*She curtsies*) Please to meet you!
Geni (*to Aladdin*) What's your desire?
Aladdin   Oh, something, *please*, to eat!
  Bring me at once a nice prime joint of meat!
  With lots of gravy!
Widow Twanky   I think I'd enjoy
  A steak and kidney pud!
Wishee   A saveloy!
  With bird's-nest soup!
Widow Twanky (*haughtily*) Some salmon à la tin!
Aladdin A sheep's head!
Wishee (*haughtily*)   And some winkles, à la pin!
Geni Will that be all? No salad, poultry?—Cheese?
  Game? Entrées? Tarts? Cockles or whelks? Some oysters?
Widow Twanky   Ooh, yes please
Wishee }
Aladdin } (*haughtily*) Well done,—à la carte!
Widow Twanky (*haughtily*)   Yes, à la carte, of course!
  And see that when you bring the cart you don't forget the horse!

Geni makes a sign. Flash! A table laden with food appears

Aladdin Look at that, Ma! Grub's up!
Wishee   Laid out smart and tidily.
Widow Twanky He's right! He *is* a Genius, most decidedly!

They approach the food

There is a loud explosion

  The Vizier enters followed by Ping and Pong with a Gatling gun

Vizier Halt!

Part II, Scene 5   43

  Now, Widow Twanky, I have you in check!
Widow Twanky Go boil yourself, you alcoholic wreck!
Vizier Soho! Defied! A truce to all your prattling!
  Beware my fiery, untamed, borrowed Gatling!
  Standby for blasting anyone within!
  Our patent way of putting brokers in!
(Aladdin moves to protect his mother)

  Seize him!...*(Police seize Aladdin)*
  His Majesty has learned with deep distress
  That this boy dared to gaze on the Princess.
  He, therefore, is condemned to death at nine,——
  Unless he pays a dirty great big fine!
Aladdin How much?
Widow Twanky Pay the fine, Aladdin,—forty bob!
  Your father always did!
Ping   Ten thousand on your knob!
Aladdin Pooh! A trifle! *(He rubs the lamp)*

Flash! A bag marked "ten thousand pounds" is thrown on
                  There! The exact amount!
Vizier ⎫
Ping   ⎬ *(together)* Amazement!!
Pong   ⎭
Aladdin It's all there! No need to count!

  Vizier (with the money), Ping and Pong (with the Gatling gun) back out,
  bowing obsequiously to Aladdin

Widow Twanky That showed 'em, son!

  A laundry maid enters

Laundry Maid Here is a note, Aladdin!
Aladdin From the Princess!
Widow Twanky   Ahhhhhhh! This his heart will gladden!
Aladdin What do I read here?! Here's more cause for sorrow!
  The Emperor's decreed she weds tomorrow!
Wishee Weds? Who?
Aladdin   The Vizier's son!
Widow Twanky   Oh dear!
Wishee   Ah, well!
Aladdin For me this is indeed an awful sell!
  And for the Princess too, for here I'm told
  That for her father's debts she's being sold.
  She bids me come to her! She loves me still!
  I'll to the palace, friends, let come what will!
Widow Twanky How?
Wishee Call the Geni back, and get more cash!

Aladdin rubs the lamp

Widow Twanky Among those Chinese toffs he'll cut a dash!
  Flash! The Geni appears
Aladdin Bring rich apparel, gold, and jewels rare;
  Then to the palace we'll at once repair
  To press my suit. When suitably I dress
  I think the Emperor I will impress.
Geni Your orders to obey I will decamp.
  Should you require aught else, just rub the lamp!
  The Geni exits
Aladdin (*aside*)
  Badroulbadour, for thee I stake my head!
  My heart is thine already! We *shall* wed!
Wishee But if a real Princess you're going to marry,
  In such a shack as this you cannot tarry.
  You haven't got a house!
Aladdin That's soon decided.
  A palace, Wishee, 's easily provided.
  Guess how!
Wishee (*miming rubbing the lamp*) I think I have an inkling!
Aladdin (*rubbing the lamp*)
  Build me a splendid palace in a twinkling!
  All precious stones and marble from each nation,
  Even grander than our great "Victoria" station!
  Now just watch this!
Flash! MUSIC. They all look out into the audience
The traverse curtain closes behind them
Aladdin There now! Behold it rising!
Widow Twanky I must say that your conjuring's most surprising!
  But even so,—to wed a real Princess!
  I really couldn't ask it in this dress!
Aladdin My dearest Ma, my money's yours, and so
  When once I've built my palace, don't you know,
  You'll have a thousand dresses, jewels and such!
  Now what have you to say?
Widow Twanky Ta very much!
  Just watch me cut a dash, and lead the fashion,
  And set young bloods aflame all of a passion!
  I'll go the pace and start some scand'lous rumours,
  I'll ride a bike, and wear a pair of bloomers!
Wishee Put bets on horses, drink, and learn to swear!
  They'll take you for a lady—ev'rywhere!

Song 17:

The Stage Manager enters with the words on an easel. This can be turned into the traditional "house number" if required

Part II, Scene 6

They exit at the end of the number

SCENE 6

The Emperor's Palace

Full stage

There is a roll of drums

Abanazar enters in a green spotlight

Abanazar Aladdin has escaped without a doubt,
He had the lamp, and that would help him out.
Fool! Fool!—to leave him there,—'twas most unwise
To lose my patience,—it lost me the prize!
But if the magic lamp I cannot get
I'll have the Princess, and defy him yet!
To gain them both I'll do my best, — and more, ——
I'll do my worst! All's fair in love and war!

Abanazar exits

Gong! Music

The Vizier, Gentlemen and ladies of the court enter in procession

The Emperor and the Princess enter

Vizier Most potent, mighty Sovereign and Tycoon,
Brother of the Sun, Cousin to the Moon,
Your subjects grovel at your Imperial feet!
Emperor Well, I don't mind! They've earned themselves a treat!
My faithful subjects all!
All   Hooray! Hooray!
Emperor I'm glad to see you make this grand display.
Our Royal Coffers being low,—don't holler!—
I'll fine you all before you go, one dollar!
All Oh!
Emperor It's costly trav'lling in those foreign climes,
But rest assured we had some high old times!
I've had such a glorious time on tour.
I went away rich, but I've come back poor!

Song 18: The Man Who Broke The Bank At Monte Carlo

Emperor   I've just got here through Paris
                    From that sunny, southern shore,
                    I to Monte Carlo went,
                    Just to raise my winter's rent.
                    Dame Fortune smiled upon me
                    As she'd never done before,
                    And I won there pots of money like a gent,

Yes, I won there pots of money like a gent!
As I walked along
The "Bois Boulong"
With an independent air,
You could hear the girls declare,
"He must be a millionaire!"
You could hear them sigh,
And wish to die,
You could see them wink the other eye,
At the Man who broke the Bank at Monte Carlo!
I stayed indoors till after lunch,
And then my daily walk
To the great Tri-umphal Arch
Was one grand tri-umphal march.
Observed by each observer
With the keenness of a hawk,
I'd a mass of money, linen, silk, and starch.
I'd a mass of money, linen, silk, and starch.

The Stage Manager enters with the words on an easel. The Emperor, the Chorus, and the audience sing

All As he walked along
The "Bois Boulong"
With an independent air,
Etc., etc.

Emperor I went back to those tables
At the Monte Carlo hell,
But I couldn't win a sou,
Not from Christian or from Jew.
Dame Fortune turned her back on me
Just like a Jezebel,
But even though my debts in mountains grew,
I never failed to keep my rendez-vous!——

All And I walked along the "Bois Boulong"
With an independent air,
Etc., etc.

Repeat chorus

Emperor So! That's the reason we need L.S.D.,—
Oof!—Pieces!—Chips!—Whate'er the term may be!
We are reduced as much,—if that may be,——
As Mr Gladstone's last majority!
When one's hard up, of course, the only course is
Carefully to husband one's resources.

To the Princess

Since you're my last resource, what I must do,
My precious darling, is to "husband" you!

Part II, Scene 6

Princess Oh no, papa!
Emperor   Don't interrupt, my dear.
  We've sent a note to princes far and near,
  And you shall wed the richest of the lot.
Princess But really, dear papa, I'd rather not!
Emperor Where's this new prince you found me for the nonce?
  I don't observe him. Bring him in at once!
The Vizier claps his hands. Gong!
Princess Oh dearest Pa, don't sacrifice your child!
Emperor Now do be quiet, and don't talk so wild.
  I'm deep in debt. Although I sadly rue it,
  To keep my throne, there's only one way to it.
  You're promised to the richest prince in marriage.
  They're building now a lovely bridal carriage.
Princess (*aside*)
  How sad a lot is mine, when you consider,
  To be knocked down unto the highest bidder.
  That I wed riches is my father's will,
  But of Aladdin I am dreaming still!

Gong! Abanazar enters with attendants bearing gifts

He bows low several times to the Emperor. NB If there is hissing from the audience the gong is struck again and the Vizier cries "Silence in Court!"

Emperor You're the suitor "Abanazar"?
Abanazar   That is so.
Emperor Where from?
Abanazar   From Africa!
Emperor   Aha! (*To the Princess*) Ho! Ho!
  (*To Abanazar*) Have you got money?
Abanazar   Tons of it! Heaps! Chunks!
  Enough to load a thousand Chinese junks!
Emperor That's a good job, for we've had suitors many,
  And never one of them was worth a penny.
Abanazar I'll give the lot, sire, for your daughter's hand.
  For no repayment will I make demand.
  I love the maid, I do, and she loves me!
(*He takes the Princess's hand, which she withdraws*)
Princess How dare you, saucy fellow, make so free!
Abanazar (*to the Emperor*) If you consent——
Princess   But, Pa, I do refuse!
Abanazar (*producing a large bundle of papers*)
  —I'll give you back, sire, all your I.O.U.'s!
Emperor My wagers all went wrong. I'd have been rich
  If "Brandy'd" only won the Caesarwich!
  You crave the honour of my daughter's hand?
Abanazar If it please you! (*He bows*) Yours, humbly to command!

Emperor (*aside to Vizier*)
You've sounded him as to the ways and means?
Vizier He's rich enough to give all China beans!

Abanazar puts a huge cigar in the Emperor's mouth, and lights it with a pound note, then hands him a jeroboam of champagne

Abanazar The gold-fields of South Africa are mine,
　Of marble palaces I've twenty-nine;
　My beds and chairs are all of solid gold,
　I light cigars with bank-notes neatly rolled.
　To me the longest tradesman's bill seems short,
　My cheapest wine costs fifty pounds a quart.
　Should you still think my offer only "fair",
　There's always the odd oil-well to spare!
　Gifts from Albion your Majesty extols,
　So!—Please!—Accept this set of clockwork dolls!

Life-size clockwork "dolls" representing Harlequin, Columbine, Clown, and Pantaloon are brought on. Abanazar winds them up with a key

　From out of their Pantomime, all British made,——
　The characters of their Harlequinade!

Scene 6a

The Harlequinade

Music 18a: "Beautiful Galathea"

Opening flourish

Blossom runs on

Pantaloon, followed by Clown, runs over to between Harlequin and Columbine and separates them. Harlequin strikes Pantaloon across the behind with his magic bat, and ducks out of the way as Pantaloon turns to strike Clown by mistake. Clown turns and strikes Blossom who butts Clown in the behind and chases Clown and Pantaloon round the stage, finally tossing them each in turn off the stage. During this, Columbine has been laughing heartily. Harlequin presents her with a rose

Meanwhile, the Harlequinade setting—"Pantaloon's front door and window, and butcher's shop door and window"—have descended into position behind them

Cadenza-like passage for horn and woodwind

　Blossom sits and scratches her ear. Columbine crosses to Blossom, shakes her by the hoof and offers her the rose. Blossom goes all shy. Columbine fixes the rose to Blossom's forehead, and gives her a kiss. Blossom goes all shy again. Columbine offers her own cheek to Blossom to be kissed. Blossom rises, looks at Columbine's cheek, then looks at the audience puzzled. Harlequin whispers in her ear. Blossom registers, and goes all shy again. Harlequin repeats whisper and Blossom gives Columbine a dainty peck on the cheek,—then rolls on her back, legs in the air. Columbine tickles Blossom's tummy.

Muted strings with bass pizzicato

Blossom dozes off. Harlequin and Columbine execute a short "love" pas de deux, ending in a prolonged kiss.

Brief repeat of horn passage

Blossom rises, and with her head nudges Harlequin who ignores her and continues to kiss Columbine. Blossom nudges Harlequin again. Harlequin pushes Blossom away with one foot. Blossom pushes Harlequin with her foot.

Cymbal crash

Harlequin turns and taps Blossom with his magic bat. Blossom is frozen in mid-attitude.

Brisk allegro following crash

Pantaloon appears at his window, and tells Columbine to come in at once. Harlequin and Columbine dance off—Harlequin into the wings, Columbine into Pantaloon's house where she joins Pantaloon at the window. He admonishes her for flirting with Harlequin. Impatiently she turns her back on him and faces out of the window.

At the same time, following the cymbal crash, the Butcher appears at his window and hangs up his various wares—including a joint, a ham, a bird, and two strings of sausages

Broad counter-melody

Butcher espies Columbine, and registers that he is in love with her. He blows her a kiss, but she turns her back on him.

Repeat of brisk allegro

Pantaloon peers out of the window, sees Butcher and waves to him. Butcher waves back. Pantaloon drags the reluctant Columbine by the hand and leads her out to meet the Butcher.

Orchestral outburst

Butcher falls to his knees and clasps Columbine's hand to his heart. She snatches her hand away. He takes out his heart (cardboard prop) and offers it to her. She declines. He runs to his shop and offers her a bouquet of flowers which she rejects,—the joint, which she rejects,—a string of sausages, which she throws at Pantaloon, who hangs them round his neck,—finally he offers her the bird, which is attached by a line to a fishing-rod, held by Clown. Harlequin enters. Butcher kneels before Columbine proffering the bird. Harlequin wields his magic bat in the direction of the bird. Clown jerks his fishing rod and the bird rises from Butcher's hands and flies low over their heads and away as Clown runs off. Pantaloon and

Butcher fall flat on the ground to avoid the bird. Columbine runs into the house and straight out of the window again into the arms of the waiting Harlequin. Pantaloon and Butcher shrug to each other and exit into their house and shop respectively.

Short flute cadenza

Butcher rearranges his wares outside his shop, including the bouquet and another string of sausages, and then disappears from view. At the same time Blossom shakes her head and comes out of her trance. She spies Widow Twanky's basket, and crosses to it as if to eat the contents. The audience shouts "DON'T TOUCH!"

Waltz

Clown enters in Milkmaid's drag, carrying bucket and stool. He beckons to Blossom who shakes her head and backs away. Clown takes Butcher's bouquet and string of sausages. Hiding the latter behind his back, he waves the bouquet from side to side under Blossom's nose. Blossom follows from side to side with her head, sniffing the bouquet. She finally grabs the bouquet between her teeth and proceeds to eat it. Clown lassoes her with the string of sausages, sits on the stool, and begins to milk Blossom. Butcher enters, sees what has happened to his bouquet, and furiously kicks the stool from beneath Clown who falls to the floor. Clown offers to sell Blossom—for slaughter. Butcher agrees and fetches bag of money which he gives to Clown. Clown holds Blossom by her sausage lead while Butcher sharpens his knife.

Brisk allegro

Pantaloon, with the sausages still round his neck, enters looking for Columbine. He crosses to behind Clown and taps him on the shoulder. Clown drops his sausage lasso to brush away Pantaloon whom he mistakes for Blossom, and then grabs the sausages hanging from Pantaloon's neck and hands them to Butcher who immediately turns and tugs with his back to Pantaloon as if to haul him off into his shop. Harlequin runs in with Columbine. He takes up Blossom's sausage lead, Columbine jumps on Blossom's back, and Harlequin starts to lead Blossom away. Pantaloon strikes Butcher with one of his own joints. Butcher discovers his mistake. Clown points to the Harlequin trio making off, and Butcher and Pantaloon follow in hot pursuit. Clown runs into Pantaloon's house and emerges immediately through the window with a red hot poker to join the end of the chase poking at Pantaloon's bottom with the poker. They have all exited UR. Blossom, Butcher, Pantaloon and Clown only re-enter DR, running across the front of the stage to exit DL, and re-enter UL.

Final waltz and gallop

Butcher catches hold of Blossom's tail. Blossom stops, bends her rear legs and sits on Butcher's chest as he slides under. Pantaloon tugs at Blossom's front end, slips under her front legs as she sits on Pantaloon's chest at the front end. Clown jumps on her back in an effort to raise her and ride her away and release the trapped Butcher and Pantaloon, but she doesn't budge. He turns round to face Butcher at the rear end who holds out his hand for help. Clown puts the red hot poker into Butcher's hand. Blossom rises with Clown on her back the wrong way round. the others rise and pursue Blossom in a circle. Harlequin enters with Columbine and waves his magic bat. They all freeze. He waves it again and they each begin to sway, enchanted, to the waltz time, one at a time. Pantaloon dances with Butcher, Clown dances with Blossom, Harlequin dances with Columbine. They form a large circle round Blossom for a final tableau with Blossom in the centre.

End of the Harlequinade

Emperor Enough! Enough, my son! My daughter's yours!——
And you are hers,—my sweet Badroulbadour's!

(*To the Princess*)

My love, that is the young man you shall wed.
Princess I do not want your "young man", as I've said!
Emperor (*to Vizier*)
Just tell those other chaps they're not required!

The Vizier signals a courtier

The courtier bows and exits

Abanazar (*to the Princess*)
Courage, Princess! I long have you admired.

Abanazar takes the Princess's arm and they exit

Emperor (*to the Vizier*)
I must get money somewhere, for 'tis shocking,
At Royal doors to have the tradesmen knocking
With unpaid bills, demanding instant payment,
When I've no change,—not ev'n a change of raiment!
Vizier That Laundress Twanky won't send home the wash.
She says we owe her one and tuppence!
Emperor Bosh!
Widow Twanky (*off*) "Where is he? Where is he? Where is he?"
Vizier Talk of the Devil!
Emperor What's that bally riot?
Who is it dares disturb our royal quiet?
(*Aside*) A creditor!—I've not the smallest doubt!
Vizier It's Widow Twanky!
Emperor (*hurriedly*) Tell her that we're out!
Here,—fob her off with that basket of groceries!

The Vizier approaches the basket

Audience Don't touch!!

Widow Twanky enters, followed by Wishee, who carries a small chest of jewels

Widow Twanky Now then! Now then! Who's messin' about with me groceries? I've been looking all over for that basket!
Widow Twanky (*remembering where she is. To the Vizier*)
  Oh mighty Emperor! (*She nudges Wishee-Washee in the ribs*)
Widow }
Wishee } (*falling on their knees before the Vizier*) Salaam! Salaam!
Emperor (*studying Widow Twanky*) A walking chop-suey!
Vizier (*to Widow Twanky*) No calling names!
  I'm not the Emperor, so stop your games!
Widow Twanky Oh, sorry!
Widow }
Wishee } (*bowing as before*) False-salaam! False-s'alarm!
Vizier Silence in Court!
  Now you! Outside!
Widow Twanky I'll do nothing of the sort!
Wishee Nothing of the sort!
Widow Twanky We want to see the foreman!
Wishee The foreman!
Vizier You can't.
  Go outside and wait your turn!
Widow Twanky I shan't!
Wishee We shan't!
Widow Twanky (*aside*) There's a hell of an echo in here!
Emperor Is this the washerwoman?
Widow Twanky "Washerwoman!"—Oh!
  I've not come here to be insulted so!
Emperor Is that a fact? Where do you usually go?
Vizier Come, come, now, my good woman, go away!
Widow Twanky I'm not your good woman! Mind what you say!

The Vizier pushes Widow Twanky in the chest backwards across the stage

Vizier Will—you—please!—to—go!

Widow Twanky pushes him similarly back again

Widow Twanky No!—No!—No!—No!—No!

  The Princess and Abanazar enter

Princess But I don't *want* to marry! That will do!
Abanazar Oh, don't say that!
Princess I will, because it's true!
Widow Twanky (*aside*)
  Aladdin's Uncle! What's he doing here!?
Abanazar (*aside*)
  Aladdin's Mother! Then *he* must be near!
  She'll ruin all!
Widow Twanky (*aloud*) You wretch! Before the town
  I'll show you up, and quickly bring you down!
Abanazar My dear, good, woman, do be calm!

Widow Twanky I won't!
  I'll have my say! You see now if I don't!
Vizier This kind of thing we really can't allow.
  It's libel!
Emperor (*covering his ears*) And what's more, an awful row!
Widow Twanky I'd like to scratch him!
Vizier Now be still I say!
  This Prince our Princess is to wed today!
Widow Twanky What *he*?!
Abanazar (*defiantly*) Yes, I!
Widow Twanky You never will!
Abanazar You'll see!
Princess And so shall I! His wife I'll *never* be!
Emperor Come, come, good people! Language if you please! Our court is not the place for scenes like these.
  What is the meaning of this fearful row?
Widow Twanky It's all his fault! Yes, I'll expose you now!
  Please, Mr Emperor, hear my petition!
  That man's a thorough bad 'un,—a magician!

The Court gasps

  Don't give the dear Princess into his power,
  Or every minute you'll regret the hour.
Emperor Pooh, pooh! (*Turning from her*)
Widow Twanky Your Majesty, *my* offer hear!
Emperor *You* cannot wed my daughter!
Widow Twanky No, that's clear!
  But I've a son who loves her——
Abanazar (*aside cunningly*) Ha—ha—ha!!!
Princess Where is he? Where? Oh, send for him, papa!
Widow Twanky He's just outside—and though I say 't as shouldn't
  A finer lad in Peking find—you couldn't.
Emperor Your son is—rich?
Widow Twanky Aye!
Abanazar (*aside*) With rage I madden!
Widow Twanky His name's Eighteen, and his age Aladdin!

Widow Twanky double-takes on herself

Emperor Where is he? What is he?—this—what's his name?
  Why's *he* not here to press his suit and claim?
Widow Twanky Wishee! Present our gifts before all eyes!
Wishee Right, Mum! ... Your Highness?

Wishee presents a jewel box to the Emperor. Roll of drums. The Emperor opens the box. MUSIC STING! Shaft of light on jewels

Widow Twanky How's that for a surprise?
Princess Oh, pa! How lovely! What a pretty sight!
Emperor If real they'll pay the National Debt outright!

Princess Aladdin wealthy! Oh, I am so glad!
Vizier I always had a liking for the lad!
Abanazar Sold! Sold! Defeated!
Emperor   Widow! Where's this son
  That shines so brightly?
Abanazar   Curses! I'm undone!   Ahhhhhh!!

Abanazar exits in a fury

Trumpets off. Gong!

Herald A noble prince approaches. Without he has been waiting.
Princess 'Tis he! 'Tis he!
Widow Twanky Well, now you'll see! His own cause he'll be stating!

Fanfare

  Aladdin enters resplendently dressed

Widow Twanky Come in, my boy. Address your sovereign do.
Aladdin I would address my sovereign's daughter too!
Princess 'Tis he!—my life, my love, my joy, my dear!
  He's going to ask you for my hand, the dear!
Aladdin Great Emperor, behold me at your throne.
  The reason why, you know. 'Tis rash I own.
  My wealth's unbounded and my love's no less
  For dear Badroulbadour, the fair Princess!
  Therefore, celestial one, I come before you!
Emperor (*fondling the jewels*)
  I'm very glad to meet you, I assure you!
  I'd diamonds once like these, aye, and carbuncles,
  But now "Oh my prophetic soul, my uncle's!"
Aladdin My liege, I'm rich beyond all comprehension,
  My treasures are too numerous to mention.
Emperor But will you promise not to bet or gamble,
  And from your fireside you will never ramble,
  And also promise me that when you wed
  You'll bring her dad a cup of tea in bed,
  To keep from swearing, not to smoke or chew?
  You swear all this—my child I'll give to you!
Aladdin If this fair maiden such an oath secures,
  My promise and my treasure both are yours!
Emperor Enough! Take her! (*He passes the Princess to Aladdin*)
       Come, shout hip-hip-hooray!
  The wedding shall take place this very day!
All Hooray!
Aladdin My sweet Princess, my own you soon shall be!
Princess Such happiness I never thought to see.

They kiss

All Hooray!

Part II, Scene 7   55

Vizier Don't squeeze her so, young man! What are you at?
Aladdin (*apologetically*) My love! (*He steps back*)
Princess   Lor', how my heart goes pit-a-pat!
The Princess pulls Aladdin to her again, and kisses him passionately
All Hooray!
Princess I do declare "Prince", you have kissed me twice!
Aladdin It may be naughty, dearest, but it's nice!

Song 19: (*Reprise of Song 10*)

Swee-Tee and Ainchee enter dressed as bridesmaids carrying an elaborate bridal veil

They place the veil on the Princess's head during the last lines of the chorus. As the scene changes Swee-Tee and Ainchee come forward where they are left alone for the next scene

SCENE 7
In front of Aladdin's palace

A moveable cut-out upstage—(full stage)

Swee-Tee Well, everything is lovely! And happiness supreme
   Combined with love and harmony's a very pleasant theme.
Ainchee Aladdin's settled down, his conduct's most sedate,
   His influence is sought by all the heads of state.
Swee-Tee The Emperor admires him, the people love him too,
   He's thoroughly respected, though envied by a few.
Ainchee The Princess lives in married bliss after all the fuss,
   So, everyone's contented,——
Swee-Tee   Yes!——
Swee-Tee⎫ (*together*) Everyone but us!
Ainchee ⎭

Song 20: "Why Am I Always The Bridesmaid?"

Swee-Tee⎫ Why am I dressed in these beautiful clothes?
Ainchee ⎭ What is the matter with me?
Swee-Tee I've been a bridesmaid for twenty-two brides.
Ainchee For me it has been twenty-three!
Both All of those maidens we've helped off the shelf,
   No doubt it seems a bit strange.
Swee-Tee Being the bridesmaid is no good to me.
Ainchee And I think I could do with a change!
Both   Why am I always a bridesmaid,——
              Never the blushing bride?
              Ding-dong!—wedding bells
              Only ring for other girls.

But one fine day——
Oh, let it be soon!——
I shall wake up in the morning
On my own honeymoon!

Swee-Tee Twenty-two times I have been to the church,
Followed the bride down the aisle.
Ainchee Twenty-three maidens have answered "I will!"
Meaning *I* won't all the while!
Swee-Tee Twenty-two couples I've seen go away,
Just him and her on their own.
Both So many times I have wished it was me,
And have gone back to Mother alone.

The Stage Manager enters with the words on an easel. The Audience join in

All Why am I always a bridesmaid,——
Never the blushing bride? Etc., etc.
Swee-Tee I had a good chance a week or two back,
Took my young man home to tea.
Mother got playful and gave him a pinch,
Yes, pinched my new boy-friend from me.
Ainchee Being a widow she knew what to do,
No use for her to complain!
When they got married that week, if you please
Both I (She) was only the bridesmaid again!
All Why am I always a bridesmaid,—
Never the blushing bride?
Etc., etc.

At the end of the number the Stage Manager removes the easel, and Swee-Tee and Ainchee exit

Abanazar's voice is heard off, crying "New lamps for old!". Abanazar enters, disguised as a pedlar, with a huge black beard, followed by Ermintrude, the camel, who is covered with new lamps, and various other items of ironmongery

Abanazar New lamps for old! Any rags or bones,—I'll buy 'em!
New lamps for old! Come out my dears and try 'em!

Song 21: For Old Things I'm Now Exchanging

(*Singing*) For old things I'm now exchanging
Others bright and new,
See my stock on view.
Hats and coats and old umbrellas,
Anything will do!
Let me deal with you!
What is't, my dears, that you have there?
An old pot I see out of repair?
Exchange it for a new!

Ha! Ha! Ha! Ha! Ha! etc.

He turns to the audience and removes his beard

(*Speaking aside*) My passion for the Princess is now as hot as Hades!
I've always nursed a sentimental weakness for the ladies!
Once I get that lamp she's mine!—Yes mine for love and kisses!
Aladdin then shall miss his wife, and *I* shall wife his missus!

He replaces his beard and calls

Here you are my dears! New lamps for old! Who'll take 'em?
Why bless my soul they're cheaper yet than anyone can make 'em!

The Princess enters, with Swee-Tee and Ainchee, minus their bridal headgear

(*Aside*) 'Tis she! 'Tis she!
Swee-Tee   Oh Princess, here's a lark!
This foolish pedlar will not make his mark.
He's got a stock of lamps as bright as gold,
He's giving them away, new lamps for old!
Princess Well, come to think of it, *we*'ve such a lamp.
I'll try for fun to change it with this tramp.

The girls giggle

(*To Ainchee*) Go fetch that old one from the second floor,
You'll find it in my room behind the door.

Ainchee exits quickly

Aladdin will be pleased, for now he'll see
He's found a treasure of a wife in me!
Abanazar (*aside*)
She don't suspect! The lamp is mine at last!
And with its aid I'll soon revenge the past!
Little does she guess how shrewd my trade is.
She too is mine! I'm partial to young ladies!

Ainchee enters with the lamp, which she gives to the Princess

Princess Well, here you are then. It's a trifle dusty.
I'll have it polished up.

She makes as if to wipe it with her sleeve

Abanazar (*snatching the lamp from her*) I *like* 'em musty!
(*Aside*)
Success at last! I'll not have long to wait!
Princess Your conduct's rude!
Abanazar   Yours will be rued too late!
Princess What do you mean?
Abanazar   Just this my fair patrician——
That I am Abanazar, the magician!——

Aladdin's foe, my sweet Badroulbadour!
I owe him much, but I'll rub out the score!

A roll of drums. He holds the lamp aloft

Mine! Mine at last! (*Chord*) Joy! Joy!
(*He kisses the lamp*)

Princess   The man's gone mad!
Swee-Tee⎫ (*huddling together*) I'm frightened!
Ainchee ⎭
Abanazar (*rubbing the lamp*)   Now you've been really had!

Flash! The Geni of the lamp appears

Princess ⎫
Swee-Tee ⎬ (*Together*) Oh, mercy! What is this?
Ainchee ⎭
Abanazar   Just wait! You'll quickly see!
(*To the Geni*)
I am your master now, slave, so attend to me.
Seize her! Bear her in! Take us to Egypt straight!
Send the palace flying. We've no time to wait.

The Geni carries the Princess into the palace upstage

Abanazar follows, and turns at the door

Goodbye, Aladdin! You've lost both lamp and bride.

Swee-Tee and Ainchee make as if to follow

Sorry! No more room! We're all full up inside!

Abanazar closes the door. Music. Roll of a drum grows to a crescendo. Smoke. The Palace rises and flies off into the air

Aladdin, Wishee-Washee and the Vizier enter

Swee-Tee (*pointing to the sky*)
Aladdin! Look!
Ainchee   Your palace!
Swee-Tee   Your Princess!
Wishee This is old Abanazar's work I guess!
Aladdin My wife! My bride!
Vizier   This is a fearful scrape!
Wishee We couldn't reach her with a fire-escape!
Vizier Here! Throw this basket at it. See if you can hit it! (*He reaches for the basket*)
Audience Don't touch!

Widow Twanky and the Emperor enter

Vizier Look! Look! The palace, flying!
Widow Twanky   I declare!
This comes of building "castles in the air!"

Part II, Scene 7

Ainchee Alas, such talk no help or comfort brings!
Vizier It comes of building palaces with wings!

All groan

Emperor You still have got the magic lamp safe?
Aladdin   No!
  It's gone up with the palace!
Vizier   Here's a go!
Emperor My debts are still unpaid.
Vizier   That's very true!
Emperor Creditors dun me, and now I'm done by you!
  Prepare to lose your head!
Widow Twanky (*swooning*) Oooooh!
Aladdin   There, Ma! Steady!
  With grief, I fear, I've lost my head already.
Vizier What ho without!

Ping and Pong enter

  Bind fast that swindling pair!
  Cast them in a cell that's furthest from the air!
Emperor Unless within an hour my child is here,
  You lose an eye, a finger, and an ear!
Widow Twanky Oh, what a nice old gent!
Aladdin   What *can* I do??
Emperor If longer time expires—then so do you!
  Tomorrow morn before the birdies sing
  My Parkhurst gibbet both your necks shall wring!
Swee-Tee ⎫ (*Aside*)
Ainchee ⎭ This cruel blow most strikingly doth prove
  The course of true love never did run smooth!
Aladdin I'd quite forgotten!!!
All   What??
Aladdin   The very thing
  In such a crisis is to rub the ring!
(*He takes the ring from his finger*)
Widow ⎫
Wishee ⎭ The magic ring will save us! Happy thought!
Aladdin (*rubbing the ring*)
  That wizard in his own trap shall be caught!

Flash! The Geni of the ring appears

Geni Your will, O Master?
Emperor   Who the deuce are you?
Geni Slave of the Ring, old party! How d'ye do!
Aladdin Good Geni, I am in a sorry plight.
  My wife and palace both have taken flight,
  'Tis Abanazar's work. His game I'd spoil,
  And all his plots and schemes of discord foil.

Geni Your palace we must follow through the air!

(*He claps his hands*)

   And so my aerial carpet I'll prepare.

Slave girls enter with a magic carpet which they unroll

   The latest model, and the best it's reckoned.
   Its speed is great—one thousand miles a second!
   Pray climb aboard, all in a row to stand,
   And in a trice I'll blow you from this land.
Aladdin Oh, many thanks! (*To others*) Hi, come on all of you.
Widow Twanky We'll I'll be blowed!
Wishee   Right!
Emperor   Here's a how d'you do!
Aladdin Quick! Climb aboard!
Emperor   I fear I'm rather heavy!
Widow Twanky You are indeed! And most impatient—very!
   (*To Geni*) Now don't go faster than sound—we may want to talk!
Geni Now close your eyes. You mustn't try to see.
   You're ready now?
All   We are!
Geni Then, one,—two,—three!!

Geni blows. Sound of a mighty wind

Black-out

                    SCENE 8
Pursuit of the flying palace through the air

           Music 21a: "Ride of The Valkyries"

Behind a gauze, and before a black curtain studded with stars, whirling comets, and the moon, we see a model of Aladdin's palace flying from one side of the stage to the other through the air, followed by a model of Aladdin, Widow Twanky, Wishee-Washee, the Emperor, The Vizier, Swee-Tee, and Ainchee on their magic carpet

Black-out

                    SCENE 9
Inside Aladdin's palace, in Africa

There is a view of the Pyramids through a window at the back. The Princess is discovered inside a tall narrow circular golden cage (like a bird's cage), surrounded by goblins, two of whom could be played by Ping and Pong

Abanazar enters

Abanazar (*aside*)—Aha!!
My plot's succeeded!—save in one particular,——
I can't obtain Badroulbadour's auricular!
The deafest ear she turns to all my speeches,
And drowns my vows of love with agonising screeches!

Abanazar approaches the Princess. She gives a little shriek. He unlocks the cage

Now don't look cross, and don't let me alarm you.
I pledge my word I don't intend to harm you.

Abanazar pulls the Princess out of the cage

But still you must be mine!
Princess   I'd rather die!
Abanazar My sweet, I long for you! I weep! I sigh!
Princess Where have you taken me?
Abanazar   Well, mia cara,
We are in Africa! Look! There's Sahara!
Princess Unhand me, vile magician! Quit my sight!
Abanazar Such words from sweet lips don't sound polite!
Will nothing please you? Issue your commands.
I'm but a baby in my darling's hands!
Princess Send for Aladdin!
Abanazar   Ah, the boon you crave
Cannot be granted. Peaceful in his grave
He lies.
Princess Not dead!
Abanazar   Alas!
Princess   I don't believe you!
We've left him but an hour!
Abanazar I'd not deceive you. Aladdin's dead! But you're not on the shelf.
Princess He can't be dead!
Abanazar   He told me so himself!
I'll make a splendid husband!
Princess   Not to me!
I'd rather die first!
Abanazar   Well, sweet, we shall see.

He returns her to the cage and locks it

I'll leave you now to make your mind up, and
Your answer must be "yes". So understand!

He crosses to the exit, then turns

Should pedlars come, and ask you if you won't
Exchange old lamps for new ones,—I say "Don't!"
Ha! ha! ha! ha!

He exits

Princess Aladdin! Oh, Aladdin! Where are you?
You are not dead! This tale cannot be true!
There's something here (*placing her hand on her heart*) that tells me I shall see
Your face again, and you will set me free!

The Princess sings with goblin chorus

Song 22:

The Stage Manager enters with an easel and the words. Princess, goblins, and audience sing

Goblins exit weeping

Princess Can it be true that my brave lad is dead?
And am I widowed but a short week wed?
Aladdin (*calling; off*) Badroulbadour! Badroulbadour!
Princess That voice! 'Tis he!—That mellow upper G
Proclaims he lives, and lives alone for me!

Aladdin appears at the window, followed by Widow Twanky, Emperor, Wishee-Washee, the Vizier, Swee-Tee, and Ainchee

Princess Belovèd!
Widow Twanky Oh, Daughter!
Emperor My child!
Wishee My life!
Swee-Tee } Our mistress!
Ainchee
Vizier My Princess!
Princess My husband!
Aladdin My wife!
Princess It's really you, Aladdin, well I never!
Aladdin To come so quickly you'll admit was clever!

They kiss

Vizier We must move quickly to avert disaster!

Aladdin and Princess continue to kiss . . .

Widow You do not kiss her quick enough. Kiss faster!

Aladdin and Princess stop kissing

Aladdin My darling, there's no moment to be lost
If this warm meeting's not to prove a frost.
I have a plan. I'll tell you what I mean.
You see this bottle? (*He produces a phial*)
Vizier Poison!
Aladdin No! Morphine!
A simple sleeping draught his games to stop.
When he gets careless just you pour a drop

Part II, Scene 9   63

    Into his lemonade, or beer, or tea,—
    Whate'er his favourite tipple chance to be.
Princess (*taking the phial, dramatically*)
    If this be crime, with crime my soul I'll saddle!
Wishee Hist!! Someone's coming!
Widow   Quick! Let's all skedaddle!
    They all exit except Princess and Aladdin, who kiss again. Aladdin then follows the others off
Princess Now help's at hand I feel as glad can be.
    Wherever can that wicked monster be?
    Oh! Here he comes! So now to test their plan,
    And try some poison on this bogey man.

Eastern dance music off

    Abanazar enters, drunk, and carrying a bottle and goblet, which he puts down as he approaches the Princess. He is followed by the drunken goblins who also stagger about the stage

Abanazar Pardon Princess, if I have kept you waiting!
    This wine is most exhil-il-il-erating!

(*He unlocks the cage*)

    Come now, my dearest, come and kiss me do!
    I wouldn't be so proud if I were you!
Princess (*pretending to be amorous*)
    To me your fatal charms are far too strong!
    They quite upset my feelings! (*She puts her arms round his neck*)
Abanazar   May I be hung!—
    But now you're talking sense! (*Aside*) She has relented!
    (*Aloud*) I see, my dear, you've changed your mind,—repented!
    I feel so gay! I want to jump and prance!
    Come, duckie, come!—and join me in a dance!

They dance a few bars—Abanazar very unsteadily. During the dance the Princess empties the contents of the phial into the goblet. Abanazar drinks from the goblet, as do the goblins behind his back

Abanazar Good gracious, what's the matter with my legs?
    They want to dance all sorts of ways, ifegs!
    Oh, glory be, what is this funny feeling?
    The ground is waltzing, and my brain is reeling!

He falls in a swoon, as do the goblins. The Princess seizes the lamp from Abanazar's girdle

Princess My spirits rise. He is intoxicated.
Abanazar My pate is dizzy!
Princess   Yes! You're dizzy-pated!
Abanazar Help! Help! Something—quick!—to eat!! (*He reaches for Widow Twanky's basket ...*)

Audience Don't touch!!

Widow Twanky enters with a rubber rolling-pin, followed by Aladdin, Emperor and the Court

Abanazar Hello, what's this?
Aladdin Your ultimate defeat!
Widow It means you're up a tree!
Abanazar (*seeing Widow Twanky*) It's Jeannie with the light brown teeth!
Widow Oh, yes! Sharp as a tack, aren't we?—you dirty old Mandarin! Anyone got an 'ammer?
Abanazar I'll kill you all!
Widow (*thumping him on the head*) Well, just take that from *me*!
Vizier My lord, let's have him strung to some tree top
So we can see his ugly carcase drop!
Abanazar Oh, mercy! Mercy! Pardon, I entreat!
Behold me kneeling humbly at your feet!
Emperor Silence, you rogue! Quick! Lock them up I say!
We'll execute this lot without delay!

Aladdin, Wishee-Washee and the Vizier seize Abanazar and push him in the cage. Widow Twanky, Swee-Tee, and Ainchee surround the goblins

Goblins Oh, gracious Princess! Don't your slaves be hard on!
We do entreat you, grant us all your pardon!
Emperor Oh, that's all kid! D'you take me for a dunce?
Off with their heads!
Princess Oh, Father dear, for once
Extend your pardon on these wicked men,
And make them mend their ways a bit, and then
Perhaps they will become in time respected.

One goblin has risen drunkenly to his knees

Widow That's more than they could ever have expected!
(*She thumps the goblin on the head. He collapses to the ground*)
Emperor Well, I don't know. Aladdin, what say you?
Aladdin He's acted very badly, that is true,
But as it's Christmas time I think that we
Must fain forgive him,—but conditionally!
Emperor You hear that now? Although our faith's been shaken —
Widow (*thumping goblins on the head*)
Just thank your lucky stars *you've*!—*saved*!—*your*!—*bacon*!
Princess And now, let's leave this dreadful place, and go
Back to our home in China, don't you know.
Aladdin Quite right, my dear! The slave I'll summon,
Although, I warn you, he's a rum 'un!

He rubs the lamp. The Geni appears behind Aladdin, who looks out front for him, waving his hand over the lamp

Aladdin Hi! Presto! Pass! Come on!...Appear!

Geni All right, my lord, your slave is here!
Aladdin Back again in China we would hook it,
So put the Palace back from where you took it!
Geni Your will I must obey. A chord please,—in the minor!

Music

The Geni claps his hands. Flash! Cymbal crash. All stagger

Swee-Tee⎫
Ainchee⎬ I can feel the palace moving!
Wishee All change for China!

Lights flicker across the stage. A vertical diorama rolls slowly downwards outside the window, depicting the Pyramids which slowly descend out of sight, followed by clouds coming down into view, giving the illusion of the Palace rising

Song 23: Oh, Abanazar (to the tune of "Oh, Mr Porter")

Widow What a shock to see fly off Aladdin's Palace grand!
Wishee Like there's been an improvement scheme slapped on our piece of land!
Widow The neighbours might have thought that we lived in a city slum!
Vizier Just scheduled in a Bill to make the Treasury look glum!
Emperor I thought there'd been an eviction for non-payment of the rent!
Vizier Were that so you'd get a "Small Commission" from Parliament!
Aladdin With the Princess let's decamp,
Genius of our Magic lamp!
All Didn't want to go but still we're glad we went!

All Oh, Abanazar, what a thing to do!
Flying us all to Africa,
Without changing at Timbuctoo!
Let's get back to China
As quickly as we can!
Oh, Abanazar, you were such a naughty man!

All Oh, Mr Geni, now it's up to you!
Please fly us out of Africa
Without changing at Timbuctoo!
Take us back to China,
As quickly as you can,
Oh, Mr Geni, you are such a clever man!

SCENE 10

Outside the Palace

The Palace is now bedecked with garlands and flags

Widow Twanky, Wishee-Washee, Swee-Tee, Emperor, the Vizier, Aladdin, Princess, and the Geni of the Lamp emerge from the palace

Widow Twanky We're home! We're home! Well, that's beyond my wits!
Wishee It knocks our trams and buses into fits!
Vizier Electricity's not in it! I never went so fast!
Widow Twanky Well anyway, I'm glad we're back in old Peking at last!
Emperor And so our darling daughter is once more to us restored.
   But where's your treasure, Son-in-law?
Aladdin   It is all safely stored.
   In fortune's sunshine, sire, again we're basking,
   You can have all you want—just for the asking.

(*He shows the lamp*)

   Badroulbadour and I, with your permission,
   Will celebrate with promptest expedition.
Emperor But where's that wicked man with schemes so deep?
Vizier I last beheld him snoring, fast asleep.
Princess He drank too deeply from his loving cup!
Emperor I think it's time, then, he was woken up.
   Although with him no more I wish to parley,
   We cannot leave him out of the Fin-arle!

Sound of a small brass band off stage

Wishee Stand by, folks! Out of the way we must move!
   We're having a visit from General Booth!

Abanazar, Ping and Pong dressed as Salvationists, and carrying instruments, with Ainchee and one other Salvation Army girl enter

Abanazar My friends! My friends! The Truth you must believe!
Widow Twanky Hello, who's this??
Emperor   Unless my eyes deceive
   Me, it's the Wicked Wizard!
Vizier   I'll give that confirmation!
Princess Great goodness, what a change!
Aladdin   Yes! Quite a transformation!
Abanazar I've seen the "light" at last!
                                 (*Aside*) This is my latest lurk!
Ping 'Tis better far to "come rejoicing"——
Pong   Than have to go to work!

Ping gives Pong a quick nudge. They hold out their collection boxes

Vizier Don't bother us, you villains, if you please!
   No! Not one bean! If you went on your knees!
Wishee Here, is it true that you save wicked women?
Ping Certainly it's true we save wicked women!
Wishee Well save us a couple for Saturday night!

Swee-Tee jabs him in the ribs

Abanazar ⎫
Ping   ⎬ (*Chanting*) We promise, sirs, to do good we'll contrive!
Pong   ⎭   Pray, brothers, let's commence—Hymn one-two-five!

Part II, Scene 10

Aladdin Oh, no! Geni!!

The Geni makes a magic pass. Flash! The Salvationists freeze, mouths open, poised to sing or blow their instruments

Geni Now Virtue reigns triumphant. Vice has passed away.
So peace, love and prosperity's the order of the day!
Aladdin But stay! Our company is not complete.
(*Pointing to his finger*)
Without this ring I should have known defeat.
(*Rubbing the ring*)
Where's she who aided me?

Flash! Geni of the Ring appears

Geni   Not far away!
And there's an extra feature to our play——
Should the gas men strike again and rob us of our light,
No need to call the army in,—our Lamp will set us right!

Aladdin raises the lamp triumphantly and rubs it. The stage is illuminated with dozens of fairy-lights

Emperor I've married off my daughter very well.
Widow Twanky I think my boy's all right, but time will tell.
Wishee Well, here's more "hitching"! 'Far as I'm concerned
I think I too a Peking Bride have earned!
(*To Swee-Tee*) Do you agree the Nuptial Knot to splice?
Swee-Tee (*in rapture*) I do!

Wishee and Swee-Tee kiss

Wishee
Swee-Tee } (*together*)   It may sound "knotty", but it's nice!
All Oooooooh! (*They cover their ears*)

Ping and Pong are arm in arm with Ainchee and another Salvation Army girl

Ping } (*together*) And we have found these maidens fair to win.
Pong }   We'll marry them,—or else we'll run them in.
Widow Twanky This talk of marriage makes me feel so giddy!
(*Sobbing*) I can't forget that I am still a "widdy"!
Others Ahhhhhhhhhhh!
Wishee (*to audience*) Ahhhhhhhhhhh!
Audience Ahhhhhhhhhhh!
Princess Now, Daddy, if you took her for your wife,
You could be nice and comfy all your life!
Aladdin She'd darn your socks, and keep you neat and tidy.
Wishee She'd never ask for money on a Friday!
Princess Come on, papa! Why don't you make Widow Twanky your Empress? There isn't anyone *else* is there?

Emperor (*staring at Widow Twanky*) There *must* be!...
  (*He turns coy and shy*) Oooooh, I don't know!
Aladdin (*to the also "coy" Widow*) Come on, Mum! Don't be shy!
Princess You both could make your minds up if you try!
Widow Twanky (*shyly*) I feel all hot and bothered!
Wishee You may be hot but you'll never be bothered!
Widow Twanky I don't know what to say!
Aladdin   Well, we can guess!
Princess It won't be "No" I'm sure.
Emperor ⎫ (*Loudly to others*) No!!
Widow ⎭   (*shyly to each other*)...YES!!

Emperor and Widow Twanky hold hands. All cheer. Fanfare!

Lamp Geni Our tale is ended, and to fairy lore
  Aladdin and his Lamp we now restore.
Ring Geni May his Arabian Nights bring happy dreams,
  And many more delightful Christmas themes.
Princess With my dear husband I may share a throne,
  But in my heart he'll ever reign alone.
Abanazar I have reformed, my wicked ways put right,
  Though I'll be just as bad tomorrow night!
Emperor We fondly hope that all the coming years
  Will bring you laughter and a lack of tears.
Wishee Prosperity and health, good friends and true,—
Swee-Tee Love and caresses,—this we hope for you!
Princess What's more, we hope—'tis for ourselves this time
  That we have pleased you with our pantomime.
Aladdin And so our story ends, as stories should,
  The moral of it's quickly understood——
Widow Stick to your luck, or else you may decamp!
Aladdin And don't forget Aladdin and his Lamp!

Song 24: (*Reprise of Song 10*)

CURTAIN

FURNITURE AND PROPERTY LIST

PART I

Scene 1

On stage: Nil

Scene 2

On stage: 2 doors marked as in text
Laundry chute
1 window (practical)
Notice marked as in text
Large box containing tacks (imaginary)
Shop signs
Laundry basket. *In it:* Laundry
Victorian pillar box

Off stage: Words of Song No. 2 chorus on easel **(Stage Manager)**
Words of Song No. 5 chorus on easel **(Stage Manager)**
Shopping basket (on stage throughout) **(Widow Twanky)**. *In it:* bags of sweets
Words of Song No. 6 chorus on easel **(Stage Manager)**
Catapult **(Wishee-Washee)**
Long scooter **(Ping and Pong)**
Torch **(Stage Manager)**
Princess' palanquin
Words of Song No. 10 chorus on easel **(Stage Manager)**
Chains **(Ping and Pong)**

Personal: **Laundry pickets:** 3 placards
Widow Twanky: bottle of gin, handkerchief
Pong: large long boots, truncheon
Ping: notebook, whip
Abanazar: flower, bouquet of flowers, bowler hat, business card

Scene 3

On stage: Backcloth with waterfall painted on it
Cave entrance (practical)
Huge boulder

Off stage: Nil

Personal: **Ermintrude:** travelling pack

Scene 4

On stage: Dragon's head. *In it:* magic lamp
Model spiders, spiders' webs
Chests of gold and precious stones (imaginary)
Jewel-bedecked trees

Off stage: Nil

Personal: **Aladdin:** ring (worn throughout)

After Geni has made a magic sign on page 33

Strike: Cave background

Set: Cave background

Set: Effigy of Queen Victoria, diarama-roll representing cascading water

PART II

Scene 5

On stage: Washing machine. *In it:* wooden flag with notice on it as in text, 1 imitation dead cat and several imitation dead fish. *On it:* huge lever
Window (practical)
An entrance upstage
Twisting panel in the upper wall
Large skip of clothes: *In it:* list, pair of knickers (with one leg), vest with holes, bloomers with a label, pair of combs, various items of clothing, bright-coloured socks
Ironing-board (as in text)
Huge mangle
Table
Cut-out of Wishee-Washee, cut-outs of Ping and Pong

Off stage: Large soup tureen and several ladles **(Wishee-Washee)**. *In it:* a pair of overalls
Long chimney-sweep brush **(Wishee-Washee)**
Huge iron **(Wishee-Washee)**
Gatling gun **(Ping and Pong)**
Bag marked "£10,000" **(Stage Manager)**
Words of Song No. 17 chorus on easel **(Stage Manager)**

Personal: **Ping and Pong:** whistles
Aladdin: magic lamp

After Geni makes a magic sign on page 42

Set: Table laden with food

Aladdin and his Wonderful Lamp 71

Scene 6

On stage: Nil

Off stage: Words of Song No. 18 chorus on easel **(Stage Manager)**
Gifts for Emperor **(Abanazar's attendants)**
Large bundle of papers **(Abanazar)**
Huge cigar **(Abanazar)**
Jeroboam of champagne **(Abanazar)**
Key **(Abanazar)**

Scene 6a

On stage: **Pantaloon's** front door and window. *In it:* red hot poker
Butcher's shop cut-out

Off stage: A joint, ham, a bird and 2 strings of sausages **(Butcher)**
Knife and a sharpener **(Butcher)**

Personal: **Harlequin:** Magic bat, rose
Butcher: cardboard heart, bouquet of flowers
Clown: fishing rod

At the end of the Harlequinade on page 51

Off stage: Small chest of jewels **(Wishee-Washee)**
Bridal veil **(Swee-Tee and Ainchee Nice)**

Scene 7

On stage: Movable cut-out of Aladdin's palace

Off stage: Words of Song No. 20 chorus on easel **(Stage Manager)**
Rolled-up carpet **(Slave Girls)**
Lamp **(Ainchee)**

Personal: **Ermintrude:** new lamps, ironmongery items
Aladdin: lamp
Abanazar: black beard

Scene 8

On stage: Black curtain studded with stars
Whirling comets
Moon
Model of **Aladdin**'s palace
Models of **Aladdin, Widow Twanky, Wishee-Washee, Emperor, Vizier, Swee-Tee, Ainchee-Nice** on magic carpet

Scene 9

On stage: Window. *Behind it:* movable pyramids
Circular golden cage

Off stage: Words of Song No. 22 chorus on easel **(Stage Manager)**
Phial **(Aladdin)**
Bottle and a goblet **(Abanazar)**

Personal: **Abanazar:** key
Widow Twanky: Rolling-pin

Scene 10

On stage: As scene 7 with garlands and flags

Off stage: Nil

Personal: **Aladdin:** lamp
Ping and Pong: musical instruments, collection boxes

LIGHTING PLOT

Property fittings required: nil

Various interior and exterior settings

PART I, SCENE 1

To open: General exterior lighting downstage
Bright green flash

Cue 1	**Abanazar** exits *Lightning effect*	(Page 3)
Cue 2	**Abanazar** exits. Thunder. Lightning *Black-out*	(Page 3)

PART I, SCENE 2

To open: Fade up from previous scene

Cue 3	**Pong:** "Of foes you have no fear." *Black-out*	(Page 12)
Cue 4	**Wishee:** "... raise left hand ..." *All lights come on, including front of house*	(Page 13)
Cue 5	**Wishee** and **Stage Manager** exit *Stage lights return to pre-black-out setting* *Front of house lights fade out*	(Page 13)
Cue 6	**Abanazar:** "... Or turn night into day." *Lights go on and off*	(Page 14)
Cue 7	**Abanazar:** "I can summon lightning up." *Flash of lightning*	(Page 14)
Cue 8	**Vizier** chases **Ping** and **Pong** and they all exit *Black-out*	(Page 24)

PART I, SCENE 3

To open: General daylight effect downstage

Cue 9	**Abanazar:** "... with a bright green lime!" *Lights turn green*	(Page 27)

Cue 10	**Audience:** "Sesame!!" *Lightning effect*	(Page 27)
Cue 11	**Abanazar:** "Ha! Ha!" *Lightning effect*	(Page 28)
Cue 12	Lightning effect *Black-out*	(Page 28)

PART I, SCENE 4

To open: General interior lighting. Lights slightly dimmed

Cue 13	Echo: "Descend!" *Lights fade up on chests of gold and rest of the cave*	(Page 29)
Cue 14	**Geni** makes a magic sign *Fade up to a brilliant daylight effect*	(Page 33)

PART II, SCENE 5

To open: General interior lighting

Cue 15	Policemen blow their whistles—comic chase *Flashing lights*	(Page 38)

PART II, SCENE 6

To open: General interior lighting full stage

Cue 16	**Abanazar** enters *Green spot on* **Abanazar**	(Page 45)
Cue 17	The **Emperor** opens the jewel box *Shaft of light on jewels*	(Page 53)

PART II, SCENE 7

To open: General exterior lighting downstage

Cue 18	**Geni** blows *Black-out*	(Page 60)

PART II, SCENE 8

To open: General exterior lighting

Cue 19	**Aladdin**'s palace flying across the stage *Black-out*	(Page 60)

PART II, SCENE 9

To open: General interior lighting

Cue 20	**Wishee:** "All change for China." *Lights flicker across the stage*	(Page 65)

PART II, SCENE 10

To open: General exterior lighting

Cue 21	**Aladdin** raises the lamp and rubs it *The stage is illuminated with fairy lights*	(Page 67)

EFFECTS PLOT

PART I

Cue 1	To open SCENE 1 *Bright green flash with smoke*	(Page 1)
Cue 2	**Dragon**'s head appears *Smoke belching from Dragon's mouth*	(Page 1)
Cue 3	**Abanazar:** "Open Sesame!" *Thunder*	(Page 2)
Cue 4	**Abanazar** exits *Thunder*	(Page 3)
Cue 5	At the end of Song No. 2 chorus *Fanfare. Gong!*	(Page 5)
Cue 6	At the end of Song No. 4 chorus *Steam, loud explosion*	(Page 7)
Cue 7	**Aladdin** emerges from the door marked "Exit" *Large clouds of steam billow out*	(Page 10)
Cue 8	**Abanazar:** "I can shoot the moon." *Sound of shots and whistle*	(Page 14)
Cue 9	**Abanazar:** ". . . The mighty thunder too." *Thunder*	(Page 14)
Cue 10	**The Princess** steps out of the palanquin *Gong!*	(Page 19)
Cue 11	**Abanazar** makes a magic sign *Flash*	(Page 23)
Cue 12	**Abanazar:** ". . . don't forget the thunder!" *Distant rumble of thunder*	(Page 27)
Cue 13	**Aladdin:** ". . . doing now I wonder?" *Roll of drums*	(Page 27)
Cue 14	**Audience:** "Sesame!!" *Thunder*	(Page 27)
Cue 15	**Abanazar:** ". . . this Wizard cut a shine!" *Thunder*	(Page 28)
Cue 16	**Aladdin** reaches for the lamp in **Dragon**'s mouth *Puff of smoke and fire belches from Dragon with a roar*	(Page 30)
Cue 17	**Abanazar:** "Too late!" *Crack of thunder*	(Page 31)

Aladdin and his Wonderful Lamp   77

Cue 18	**Aladdin:** ". . . death's cold hand shall sever."	(Page 31)
	Hissing noise	
Cue 19	**Aladdin:** "I'll rub it on my sleeve!"	(Page 32)
	Flash	
Cue 20	**Spirits:** ". . . You're free!" **Geni** makes a magic sign	(Page 33)
	Thunder	

PART II

Cue 21	At the end of Song No. 14 chorus	(Page 34)
	Factory hooter	
Cue 22	At the end of Song No. 15 chorus	(Page 36)
	Factory hooter	
Cue 23	**Wishee-Washee** starts the washing-machine	(Page 36)
	Steam, terrible banging noise	
Cue 24	**Widow Twanky** closes machine lid and pulls the lever	(Page 37)
	Steam, terrible banging noise	
Cue 25	After **Widow Twanky** has ironed 2 or 3 items	(Page 37)
	Whistle from the machine	
Cue 26	**Widow Twanky** places **Wishee-Washee** cut-out into the machine	(Page 37)
	Steam, clanking engines	
Cue 27	During the comic chase—**Widow Twanky** turns on machine	(Page 39)
	Terrible grinding noises, explosion	
Cue 28	**Widow Twanky:** ". . . aye, there's the rub!"	(Page 42)
	Flash	
Cue 29	**Widow:** ". . . don't forget the horse!" Magic sign	(Page 42)
	Flash	
Cue 30	**Widow and Wishee** approach food on table	(Page 42)
	Loud explosion	
Cue 31	**Aladdin:** ". . . a trifle." He rubs the lamp	(Page 43)
	Flash	
Cue 32	**Aladdin:** ". . . get more cash!" Rubs lamp	(Page 44)
	Flash	
Cue 33	**Aladdin:** ". . . now just watch this."	(Page 44)
	Flash	
Cue 34	To open SCENE 6	(Page 45)
	Roll of drums	
Cue 35	**Abanazar** exits	(Page 45)
	Gong!	
Cue 36	**Princess:** ". . . I am dreaming still."	(Page 47)
	Gong	
Cue 37	**Wishee** presents a jewel box to the Emperor	(Page 53)
	Drumroll. Music.	

Cue 38	**Abanazar** exits: "Ahhhhhh!" *Trumpets off. Gong!*	(Page 54)
Cue 39	**Widow:** "... he'll be stating!" *Fanfare*	(Page 54)
Cue 40	**Abanazar:** "... rub out the score!" *Roll of drums*	(Page 58)
Cue 41	**Abanazar:** "... been really had!" *Flash*	(Page 58)
Cue 42	**Abanazar** closes the door *Roll of drums grows to crescendo, smoke, palace rises*	(Page 58)
Cue 43	**Aladdin:** "... shall be caught!" *Flash*	(Page 59)
Cue 44	**Geni:** "... One,—two,—three!!" *Mighty wind blows*	(Page 60)
Cue 45	**Princess:** "... poison on this bogey man" *Eastern dance music*	(Page 63)
Cue 46	**Geni** claps his hands *Flash, cymbal clash*	(Page 65)
Cue 47	**Emperor:** "... out of the Fin-arle!" *Sound of small brass band offstage*	(Page 66)
Cue 48	**Aladdin:** "Geni!" Magic sign *Flash*	(Page 67)
Cue 49	**Aladdin:** "... who aided me?" *Flash*	(Page 67)
Cue 50	**Emperor** and **Widow** hold hands *Fanfare*	(Page 68)

www.ingramcontent.com/pod-product-compliance
Ingram Content Group UK Ltd.
Pitfield, Milton Keynes, MK11 3LW, UK
UKHW021844210426
5322IPUK00022B/457